With Their Dying Breaths:

A History of Waverly Hills Tuberculosis Sanatorium

In Louisville, Kentucky

By CC Thomas

Copyright © 2007 by CC Thomas

All rights reserved. This book or any parts thereof may not be reproduced in any form without written permission. Printed in the United States of America.

Published by CC Thomas Writing Solutions, LLC.
516 E. Chestnut St.
Corydon, IN 47112
www.iknowgoodbooks.blogspot.com

Library of Congress Cataloging-in-Publication Data

Thomas, CC
 With Their Dying Breaths: A History of Waverly Hills Sanatorium/CC Thomas.

 Includes bibliographical references.
 ISBN9781478292760 (pbk. alk. Paper)

1. History—Local Kentucky. 2. History--Tuberculosis—Hospital.

According to WHO (World Health Organization), as of 2012, one third of the world's population is currently infected with the TB (tuberculosis) bacteria.

## Introduction and Dedication

When I was first approached about writing an article for *The Capitol News* (a now defunct local newspaper) about Waverly Hills Tuberculosis Hospital, I was excited......and intrigued. Not by its infamous haunted present but by its very famous past. I am one of those people who find history fascinating and jumping headfirst into the story didn't begin to cover it.

As a Kentucky native, I had a TB hospital in my little hometown and I was shocked to learn how these two places were connected. The deeper I got into my research, the more fascinating the topic became to me. To think that a disease could so shape and change a community, a nation, and today be virtually unknown is still unthinkable to me.

So, for the next several months, I spent hours in the public library in downtown Louisville, reading literally every newspaper article that had ever been published in the area. (At one time, these items had been collected in a scrapbook but the librarians informed me it just kept getting stolen.) I poured through archival newspapers, pamphlets, brochures-you name it. I went to local historical libraries and sat in rooms wearing white gloves handling documents paper-thin and ready to crumble. I traveled countless miles researching even the vaguest hint of a story. I listened to old-timers and sons and daughters and nieces and nephews and friends of old-timers. I was hooked and I wanted to collect all the history before it became as lost as those tuberculosis victims of so long ago.

The public's desire to know more about the local landmark was strong and I partnered with owners Charlie and Tina Mattingly to write a comprehensive history of the place. The Mattinglys were kind enough to allow me access to the building and shared with me many stories of their own. Theirs is a true labor of love—restoring the hospital to its former magnificence and, perhaps, finding new uses for her. Although the Mattinglys and I parted ways, the story never left me. For years, the history has been sitting on my computer, waiting for an audience.

So, here it is-all that I could find as a researcher and writer. Surely, though, there's more. I would love to hear your story, if you can add to these pages. A history as fascinating as this one shouldn't die—it is up to the public to keep it alive.

I hope that when you read these pages, you will find the story behind the victims as fascinating as I did.

*It is to them, to the untold countless victims of tuberculosis, that I dedicate this book. I hope that all those victims from so long ago will finally have their stories heard. Finally, I hope they are remembered.

Table of Contents

Introduction and Dedication..........................4

Chapter One-      With Their Dying Breaths: A Brief History of Tuberculosis in the United States....................…..9

Chapter Two-      No Rest for the Weary: Sanatoriums in America...................…....20

Chapter Three-      Desperate Measures: Kentucky's Attempts to Cure Tuberculosis.......31

Chapter Four-      New Beginnings: The Creation of Waverly Hills Tuberculosis Sanatorium..............49

Chapter Five-      Time Heals All Wounds: Life at Waverly Hills……..…………….65

Chapter Six-      Dying to Get Well: Remedies, Cures and Treatments…………...84

Chapter Seven-      The End of an Era: The Closing of Waverly Hills………………101

| | |
|---|---|
| Chapter Eight- | A White Elephant: Life After Waverly Hills....................115 |
| Chapter Nine- | A Place to Call Home: The Buildings of Waverly Hills......................135 |
| Chapter Ten- | The Pioneers: Important Louisvillians in the Fight Against Tuberculosis............150 |
| Chapter Eleven- | A Bright Future: Waverly Hills Today...................158 |
| Chapter Twelve- | Dim Prospects: Tuberculosis Today....167 |
| | Photo Credits...........170 |

# Chapter One
# With Their Dying Breaths:
# A Brief History of Tuberculosis in the United States

If I were to ask you to imagine living through the Black Death or the Black Plague, I can imagine you would shudder in horror. Yet there is a disease much more deadly, a disease so powerful it has killed more people than all the world wars, influenza **and** AIDS. Combined. That disease is tuberculosis.

| Influenza | 178 million |
|---|---|
| Black Death | 75 million |
| Bubonic Plague | 45 million |
| AIDS | 25 million |
| Tuberculosis | 2 billion |

You've probably heard of tuberculosis. It's a disease still around today, although most new cases occur in developing nations. But we just don't worry about it anymore. Let's face it-it's easy in today's world to be sick. At the first signs of an illness, we hop down to the pharmacy or health-food store. If over-the-counter medications don't work, we seek a doctor's care and get a cure. Contracting tuberculosis simply isn't a concern for the modern man or woman living in the United States.

Being sick, though, wasn't always so easy. It's hard to imagine a world where medication couldn't solve the problem-couldn't cure the disease-but that was the case less than 80 years ago when the white plague ravaged the United States and Europe.

> Tuberculosis is a disease that has infected mankind since the earliest known times. Shown here is an Egyptian mummy who suffered from spinal tuberculosis. Ancient cultures often wrote of a disease where the victims coughed up blood. It is believed they were referring to tuberculosis.

Tuberculosis, often called the "plague of all plagues", is a contagious and deadly respiratory affliction that has been around since the earliest times. Tuberculosis is an ancient disease described by both the Greeks and Romans and was known then as *phthisis*. Tuberculosis is also one of the many diseases thought to have wiped out Native American populations, although it was one of the few diseases already on the North American continent before early colonists arrived.

Tuberculosis would come to be known by many names over the years. It was most commonly known as *consumption* because many of the victims appeared to be "consumed" by something inside their bodies and would appear to quite literally waste away. Other names for the disease were *wasting disease* and the *white plague* or *white death* because of the paleness of a victim's skin.

Tuberculosis was a major health concern in the late $19^{th}$ and early $20^{th}$ centuries in the United States and was particularly common in newly-developing urban areas where more and more of the population were moving due to the Industrial Revolution. The typical home in America at that time looked quite different than the homes of today. Most dwellings held between 7 to 10 people, many of those children. It was also not uncommon for several generations to live together under one roof, especially with so many immigrants arriving in the US with only a suitcase to their name.

In addition to more people being squeezed into smaller and smaller areas, poor sanitation, poor nutrition and lack of information about how diseases spread helped tuberculosis get a foothold and set the stage for an international disaster.

Strangely enough, though, consumption soon came to be associated with famous artists and painters of the day. This may be where the term "suffering artist" comes from. After a time, it was even somewhat admirable to have the disease,

It's hard to believe, but many Victorian women tried to dress like tuberculosis victims. It was considered chic to have the disease.

especially since so many youth were dying. It was a story both tragic and romantic. While the poor had a much higher death rate, probably due to living conditions, as the disease spread it soon came to be known as a gentlemen's disease. As the effects of early consumption were not able to be seen, carrying a delicate lace handkerchief became more of a fashion accessory than an object to deter disease.

Consumption soon became just a way of life for those living in the first part of the century. One effect of consumption was on women's fashion. Women at the time began to wear white face powder to mirror the effects of the pale complexion of TB sufferers. The high necklines would hide swollen glands and the impossibly thin waists of the dresses were due to the skeletal look of the many disease victims. In paintings from that era, many women can be seen holding flower bouquets, called tussie-mussies or nosegays. The bouquet would often hold herbs such as rosemary and lavender, plants known for their antibacterial qualities even then. Bouquets were used to mask the unpleasant smells of the day and to protect the wearer from disease.

What is this disease that so colored the lives of our ancestors but which is almost unheard of today?

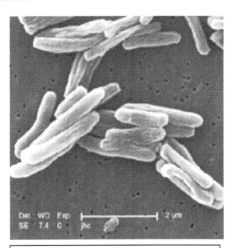

**Tuberculosis bacterium under the microscope.**

Tuberculosis is caused by a bacterium and was most often spread by water droplets as those infected coughed, sneezed, spoke or spit. In the 1800's something as commonplace as a sneeze could be lethal. One sneeze had the potential to hold 30 million droplets of moisture. Each of those droplets could hold more than 100 tuberculosis bacterium. The lightest moisture droplets were the most dangerous because the tuberculosis bacilli could float in the air, infecting whomever it came in contact with even after the moisture holding it had evaporated.

Spitting was even worse since it was such a common practice of the time, much like smoking is today. When an unsuspecting passerby stepped into infected saliva on the street, they might carry the disease home to their families on the bottom of their shoe. Even when the saliva dried, diseased particles could evaporate into the air and be carried on the wind much like the droplets in the moisture from a sneeze. At one time, there were various laws in place both in the United States and in Europe forbidding public spitting and the use of spittoons.

However, it was generally believed that tuberculosis could be contracted through hereditary traits, bad spirits in the air and odors from foul sewage, a problem for many who lived in the cities. Many also believed that a rich diet, lazy attitude and a cold climate could bring on the disease. Doctors at that time knew almost nothing about germ transmission and many seriously doubted that "tiny creatures" that lived inside the body had the potential to kill. Thus, the diagnosis was based on symptoms and visible signs.

> While tuberculosis certainly affected the poor, many famous and wealthy individuals would succumb to the disease including:
> - Poet Lord Byron
> - Stephen Crane, author of *The Red Badge of Courage*
> - Author Ralph Waldo Emerson
> - George Orwell, author of *1984* and *Animal Farm*
> - Artist Paul Gaugin
> - Composer Frederic Chopin
> - US Presidents Ulysses S. Grant and Andrew Jackson
> - First Ladies Eleanor Roosevelt and Jane Pierce
> - Florence Nightingale
> - Alexander Graham Bell
> - Vivian Leigh, the actress who brought Scarlett O'Hara to life in the film classic *Gone With the Wind*.

At a time when penicillin was still decades from discovery, tuberculosis was a disease with less than a 50% survival rate. What made it so much worse was the extremely high risk of contagion. One in three people who came in close contact with an infected person was likely to contract TB themselves.

When an individual would first contract TB, they might have confused it with other common ailments of the time. First a feeling of unwellness would begin with general aches and pains in the chest area. In the beginning of the illness, many would refuse to seek treatment for just feeling 'under the weather'. After all, the malaise could have been dozens of things, including a common cold. But, unlike other more common bacteria, TB cannot be destroyed by white blood cells. By the time a victim realized the persistent feeling could be something worse, it was often too late.

The next symptom was a persistent, dry cough. The cough would soon turn severe, most often in the morning with the phlegm, called sputum, containing either a green or yellow discharge, clear

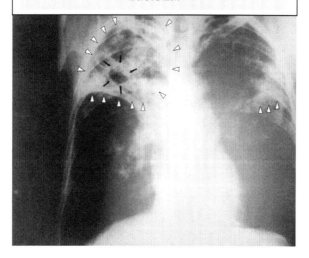

An X-ray showing advanced pulmonary tuberculosis. The effects of the disease can easily be seen within the pointing arrows and is best described as a large hole where the tissue has already been "eaten" by the bacteria.

signs of an infection. Sufferers would often have a low grade fever and would wake up in the night drenched in sweat. Eventually, a loss in appetite would occur and then a gradual weight loss, creating an unhealthy cycle.

As the disease progressed, pain in the chest would become quite common. Often throat ulcers were a result of the constant coughing and made talking and eating very difficult. Coughing up blood and extreme paling of the skin were the most visible symptoms. As the lungs became more diseased, the tissue itself would start to dissolve and would be coughed up as well. The name "tuberculosis" actually comes from the *tubercles*, little lumps that would form in affected tissues. If those holes, or lesions, were at the site of a major artery, the individual could bleed to death while coughing, some quite literally drowning in their own blood.

In some patients, the TB would carry to the lymph nodes which would become swollen and painful. This would cause an infection and pus would often seep from the neck. Another distinctive symptom of chronic TB was violent coughing fits. This was called "graveyard coughs" by doctors of the time. The end of the disease also brought severe stomach cramping and choking as sufferers struggled for oxygen.

In many patients, the disease would appear to get better although the infected party would still carry the bacteria. TB bacterium can lie dormant for long periods of time and the process of dying from tuberculosis can take months or even years. The disease returned in 50-60% of the cases.

Tuberculosis most often affected the lungs but could also affect any other body system or organ including the soft tissue of the eyes. Another common TB site was the central nervous system, a much more serious and more fatal place for the disease to strike. Those suffering from TB of the brain almost always died and were often rendered insane by the final stages of the disease. This type of TB, *Tuberculosis meningitis*, was most common in young children. Another part of the central nervous system affected was the spinal column. *Spinal tuberculosis* most often struck children and left them paralyzed. In most cases, the disease started in the lungs and then spread to other organs through the blood stream. The disease also affected the bones, the joints, the kidneys and even the reproductive organs. Advanced TB acted much like cancer spreading from one organ to another. *Tuberculosis peritonitis*, tuberculosis of the lining of the abdominal cavity, caused terrible pain to the victims and has been compared to the same pain as an appendicitis attack.

In the early 1800's in Great Britain, at least one in four deaths could be attributed to some type of TB. It would not be until the 1880's that scientists and doctors recognized that TB was a contagious disease. Even into the early 1900's in Europe, the disease had continued to claim one in every ten peoples in the population.

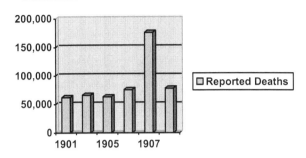

The United States was certainly faring no better than Europe during this time. In a tuberculosis registration of the 1900 United States census, it was estimated that more than 50% of the death-rate could be attributed to tuberculosis. Some estimates place this number closer to 80%. In any event, tuberculosis was the leading cause of death during this time in both the United States and Europe.

The outlook for a tuberculosis sufferer was grim. Finally, when it seemed as if nothing could stop the plague from taking over the nation, a solution was proposed: the sanatorium.

> **The real problem with obtaining accurate figures is that more than half the states in the US at that time had no adequate system of registering the dead.**

## Chapter Two
## Rest for the Weary:
## Sanatoriums in America

While there was no known cure for tuberculosis until midway through the century, a solution was offered: the sanatorium. The first sanatoriums in the nation were opened specifically to treat tuberculosis and were located in the Adirondacks and Pocono Mountains in New York State.

Dr. E. L. Trudeau opened the Adirondack Cottage Sanatorium in Saranac Lake, New York in 1885. Trudeau had long been a victim of tuberculosis and originally visited the area as a sort of last dying wish.

Instead, he found himself refreshed by the clean mountain air and started feeling better. Inspired by the change in his own health, he became convinced he had finally discovered a sort of cure for tuberculosis. He would later open the first hospital in the nation devoted entirely and exclusively to the long-term care of TB victims. However, rather

than being 'cured' of tuberculosis, Trudeau went into remission. His remission, though, would last for another 30 years before he finally succumbed to tuberculosis in 1915.

Based on his success there, combined with the successes at other clinics across the world, sanatoriums soon opened up all over the United States. It was no accident that the sanatoriums were located in mountainous areas. It was the generally held opinion at the time that the polluted city air either caused tuberculosis or most certainly made it worse. The death rate in heavily populated areas far outnumbered those from more rural areas. Thus, pure country air was thought to more quickly heal diseased lungs.

> *Sanitariums* (notice the difference in spelling) had long been in vogue in the United States and abroad. Sanitariums were health resorts and offered many different services to clients including massages and mineral baths and would be similar to today's spa and spa resorts. The most famous sanitarium in the area was located across the Ohio River in Orange County, Indiana at French Lick Springs Resort, pictured above and West Baden Springs Resort. These sulfur and mineral springs were touted for their medical benefits. In the early 20th century, celebrities from all over the United States were finding their way to this small town and a daily train route ran between French Lick and Chicago.
> A distinction was soon made between *sanitariums* (a health resort) and *sanatoriums* (a type of hospital).

However, there was another theory operating within the general public: remove the infected victims to prevent the disease from spreading further. The period of greatest infection in the US was also the period of highest immigration rates. In the latter half of the 1800's, immigrants were arriving in New York City at the rate of over 2000 each day. Unfortunately, most arrived with no money and would be forced to live in large tenement areas in the city. These tenements were widely known to have been breeding grounds for various diseases. In addition to the extremely cramped living conditions, deficient water and sewage draining, filthy streets with raw waste, polluted water supplies, generally poor ventilation and improperly constructed buildings added to the overall unhealthy aspect

Posters such as this one were very common as numerous health organizations were formed to combat both tuberculosis and another well-known killer of the time: influenza.

of most large cities. While isolation of the sick often began at home, the rate at which the infection could spread from one person to another was staggering. As the public, and doctors, learned more about how diseases spread, it soon became apparent that quarantine might be the only alternative to save the uninfected.

The first 'TB' laws came into being in the 1890's, around the

> **By 1931, there were over 1400 tuberculosis associations across the country.**

same time as the sanatoriums and the first state boards of health. Voluntary reporting was soon replaced by laws that required all persons suffering from tuberculosis to report their disease to local health officials. When the first forced mandatory notifications began, it was seen as quite controversial. Many doctors insisted it was a clear violation of doctor-patient privilege. However, public demand soon won out and health care officials nation-wide were obligated to report all cases of tuberculosis. When TB sufferers' names would appear on the rolls, their situation became a matter of public knowledge.

Soon, hysteria took over as the disease swept through the country and many TB sufferers would be treated as badly as lepers in Old Testament times. Landlords refused to rent rooms to victims while barbers refused to shave consumptive men. In some states, TB victims could not teach school. (Today, a mandatory TB test is still required to become a public school teacher in Kentucky). In

Washington State, consumptives were not even permitted to marry. If they did, they could face up to a $1000 fine and 3 years in jail. Consumptives were strongly advised not to have children as many believed the disease could be passed along genetically. Even some hospitals would discourage admitting patients with advanced cases of tuberculosis. Some families, wanting to hide their situation, would simply report that loved ones had died after "a long illness".

The sanatorium seemed like the perfect solution.

| Year | Number of TB Hospitals | Number of Beds |
|---|---|---|
| 1898 | 600 hospitals | 95,000 |
| 1935 | 466 hospitals | 49,000 |
| 1945 | 1002 hospitals | 98,000 |

For many, though, the sanatorium would be their final resting place. One study at the time noted that nearly 2/3 of sanatorium patients waited until they were undeniably sick before consulting a physician, not wanting to admit the awful truth. When a TB victim had such obvious symptoms, the disease would often be in the final stages and nothing could be done.

Unfortunately, many victims who came to sanatoriums expecting a cure would simply die there and the sanatoriums soon became little more than a "waiting rooms for death". Only about 50% of patients ever recovered or went into long-term remission.

Some sanatoriums still resembled the health care resorts and could charge for their services, thus ensuring that the wealthiest would obtain better care. The average charge rate for the nicer hospitals would vary from $8-$15 per week, at a time when an hourly wage of 15 cents an hour was considered good. Even death would be not enough of a reason for segregation in such turbulent times: white TB sufferers and blacks would be treated at different hospitals.

---

### The Hardest Job

A 1931 news article gave special directions to mothers who were caring for tubercular children in the home:

- Isolate the child in a separate room with the door closed. If child protests, install a screen or grate in the door so that child cannot leave area.
- Remove any furniture that is not essential. All items left must be cleaned with soap and water on a regular basis.
- Attach a paper bag to bedside for soiled handkerchiefs which will later need to be burned.
- Wear a mask, cap and apron every time in room and then place them in separate laundry area. Fresh clothing must be worn for each visit to room.
- Patient dishes must be kept separate and boiled in room.
- Wash hands frequently.

As more and more became ill, the need for public hospitals began to arise and the first state to establish a state-funded sanatorium was Massachusetts in 1895. As soldiers began returning from both the First and then Second World Wars, it became necessary to stop the influx of the disease on this front and the Federal Government would provide for the treatments of its soldiers and sailors at Fort Bayard and Fort Stanton in New Mexico.

New scenery was always at the top of the list for TB treatments and thousands of sufferers began moving about the United States, constantly searching for the healthiest atmosphere. The western half of the US was quite popular and it has been estimated that one in four migrants to California and one in three to Arizona moved there for the benefit of their health.

Although the types and locations of these hospitals would vary, the prevailing medical treatments were similar. The most popular and most enforced treatment involved rest and recuperation. Most tuberculosis victims were encouraged, even forced, to move about as little as possible, if at all. Doctors believed that the lungs must be kept still so that fibroid tissue couldn't take a foothold and turn into a more advanced condition. Quiet activities such as reading, writing and talking were encouraged although many sanatoriums would prevent even these simple forms of entertainment. Some sanatoriums went so far as to forbid patients to reach for objects or move their arms or body. Coughing was frowned upon because it might hamper the healing of delicate lung tissue.

Recuperation became a serious business. Nothing was permitted in the hospitals that might give the patient too much mental strain or emotional exertion. Therefore, there was quite a list of forbidden activities: no bridge, poker, whist, letter writing, chess, or playing music. If temperatures were feverish, patients might not even be allowed visitors. If visitors were allowed in the room, they were not permitted to tell the patients anything unpleasant or even mention the disease.

There was a TB hospital within a day's drive of most towns. This one in London, Kentucky has been converted into office space but still retains some architectural features of the old hospital. By 1948, Kentucky had 1600 beds for TB victims and had built six TB hospitals outside Louisville including those in Warren, Kenton, and Fayette Counties.

What was allowed for the typical patient? Reading a novel that had already been pre-approved by the nursing staff (one which did not cause the least bit of excitement or mental concentration), taking a temperature, eating as much and as often as possible, and lying on the porches watching the clouds.

In addition to rest, eating healthy was on the list for recommendations for all TB patients. The patient's daily intake was strictly monitored and a typical menu each day might include: 6-8 eggs, bouillon, peptone, salt, milk, meat, and legumes. Some foods, such as rich sauces, spices, tea and coffee, were frowned upon, though, as they had an over-stimulating effect. Many doctors encouraged their patients to eat to their fullest capacity and then beyond. For many patients, eating that much food was a big problem because many simply had no appetite or had indigestion, both common complaints of tuberculosis sufferers. Many advanced case patients also had to deal with diarrhea, which made eating any type of liquid diet problematic.

Perhaps as important as rest and diet, optimism was the key to recovery. At many hospitals, patients were absolutely forbidden to talk about their illnesses to one another. The staff felt dwelling on the situation would put the patients in morose attitudes and delay the healing process.

The buildings and rooms of patients were monitored and designed just as strictly as their diets and daily schedules. All hospital rooms were supposed to be on the south side of the building so as to receive the most direct and warming sunlight. Plenty of windows were also a must. If a patient were to heal at home, there was a list of other guidelines available that closely matched the sterile hospital setting:

- The floor in a home should have been made of wood, with no carpets or rugs that could trap the tuberculosis germs. Frequent scrubbing was considered a necessity.
- An ideal porch would extend for three sides of the house or have at least three open sides. The porch would need to be wide enough to accommodate a bed or chair. The bed or chair should be movable so that the patient could be wheeled to face the most sunlight or most direct breezes.
- The colors of an invalid's room were supposed to be light and bright so as to cheer the spirit. However, no wallpaper could be hung.
- Above all, the patients must be separated from the uninfected at all costs.
- Open, flowing air was an absolute necessity.

Focused on preventing the disease from spreading to the general public, sanitariums opted to be self-contained which included growing their own crops, husbanding their own animals for production and even institutionalizing their own schools and orphanages. Sanitariums would become worlds unto themselves as the public desperately tried to stem the rising plague. Quarantine seemed the only option.

A common feature on many turn-of-the-century homes was the 'sunporch' as seen here. Today such back porches are used for socializing. During the first part of the 20th century these rooms could be an indication that the house had a tuberculosis sufferer.

# Chapter Three
# Desperate Measures:
# Kentucky's Attempts to Cure Tuberculosis

At the beginning of the twentieth century, Louisville was still virtually a swampland and many in the area became infected with tuberculosis, cholera and other deadly diseases. Colorado was the only state in the nation that had a higher tuberculosis death rate than Kentucky for much of the late eighteenth and early nineteenth centuries. In 1910, the death rate was reaching true epidemic proportions as 13,436 cases of tuberculosis were confirmed, drastically up from the year before. Both city and county officials reported that an average year prior to 1910 included only 6500 cases. The death rate was even higher in the city. In Louisville, as many as one in every eight citizens was dying of the white plague. Newspapers at the time estimated that as many as 20,000 might have been infected. Eventually, Kentucky would surpass even Colorado and would lead the nation for many years in tuberculosis-related deaths.

With so many sick and dying from the disease, the city was faced with a true plague. What made the situation

> In 1910, Boston, Massachusetts, in a desperate attempt to stop the skyrocketing death rate, banned public drinking cups. TB, and diseases like it, was one of the primary reasons public drinking fountains and paper disposable cups were invented.

so much worse was the fact that almost all the victims were being cared for by family members, thereby infecting another generation. It seemed as if nothing could stop the vicious cycle. Newspaper reports of the time stated that suffering TB victims were "creating a menace to the health of every person". Several prominent citizens were concerned about the diseases and the high rates of infection and decided to take action. Unfortunately, the issue was quite controversial and in 1910 the first bill for establishing a sanatorium was vetoed by the governor. Kentucky was desperate to stem the tide of the growing plague.

### The First Tuberculosis Hospital in the World: The Mammoth Cave House

One of the most unusual tuberculosis experiments occurred in May of 1842 right here in Kentucky, a full 17 years before the first

Mammoth Cave is now a National Park but could be considered the birthplace of the world's first tuberculosis sanatorium.

recognized sanatorium opened in Germany in 1859. The tuberculosis experiment was the brainchild of Dr. John Croghan.

Dr. Croghan was a noted Louisville physician, son of William Croghan and Lucy Clark, a sister of the Revolutionary War hero, George Rogers Clark. Dr. John Croghan and his family owned nearby Mammoth Cave, having purchased the properties for $10,000. In September of 1842, he opened his cave to sufferers of tuberculosis. Croghan felt the uniformity of temperature (54 degrees Fahrenheit year round) and the pure, highly oxygenated air might provide the cure.

The idea was not as crazy as it might seem. The restorative properties of caves were well-known at the time and the Mammoth Cave stories seemed to be legendary in the area. Prior to Croghan owning the cave, a large force of African slaves were living and working there, mining saltpeter. Doctors noted that these men appeared to be in excellent physical condition and suffered from no illnesses, especially illnesses of the lungs. Other popular stories concern miners who were never sick and attributed their excellent health to the saltpeter, used for making gunpowder, found in the caves. Even miners and diggers who were ill when employed at Mammoth Cave were being restored to physical health by their time underground. In 1860, an area doctor wrote that the cave air could even completely heal diarrhea and dysentery. "It is not an uncommon occurrence for a person in delicate health to accomplish a journey of twenty miles in the Cave, without suffering from fatigue." It seemed like Croghan may have found the answer so desperately hoped for.

Croghan was also influenced by a congressman and doctor from Columbia, Kentucky, Nathan Gaither, and by a Louisville doctor, William McDowell, who both felt that diseases could be cured by the salt and iron properties and the constant temperature found deep inside the cave system. In 1844, Croghan wrote, "A knowledge of the curative properties of the cave air is not, as is generally supposed, of recent date. It has long been known. A physician of great respectability, formerly a member of Congress from a district adjoining the cave, was so firmly convinced of the medical properties of its air, as to express more than twenty years ago, as his opinion, that the State of Kentucky ought to

The Historic Entrance to the cave, where tuberculars would have entered.

purchase it, with a view to establish a hospital in one of its avenues." Croghan must have felt at last that he was on the right track, supported by the most influential men in Kentucky.

Dr. Croghan had expected and planned for over 100 consumptives and decided to try the experiment for one year to determine if the medicinal air in the cave could cure, or possibly lessen, the symptoms of tuberculosis. Calling it a resort for invalids, Croghan wrote in private letters, "I am convinced they would all return to the land above with greatly improved health."

> The healing properties of caves dates back to 4th century BC Chinese writing where crushed stalactites were used in cough medicines, to stop bleeding and to encourage milk production in wet nurses. Other notable historic instances include:
> - In the 1600's, Europeans used cave formations to treat broken bones, fever, eye disease, infected wounds, mange and evil spirits.
> - Gypsum has been used as a food additive in ice cream, spaghetti, baking powder, canned vegetables, jelly, cereal and beer.
> - Epsom salts have been used since the 1600's to treat aches, pains and wounds.
> - Calcium carbonate, a common cave component, is the main ingredient in Tums and Rolaids.

However, only ten consumptives signed up for

the progressive treatment, a number far below what Croghan had hoped for.

After the failed experiment, Croghan would retire to his family home, Locust Grove in Louisville. He would die from tuberculosis just six years after the Mammoth Cave experiment.

Two stone cottages were built inside the cave along with ten frame cottages, each of which stood approximately 30 feet apart. The cottages measured 12 feet by 18 feet and had canvas ceilings. Stoves were placed inside these structures for heat and general cooking purposes. The first stone house located inside the cave was Dr. Croghan's office and the second one was used as a dining room. Croghan, himself a TB victim, did not live in the cave with the other patients but instead had a small cabin built at the entrance. He situated his cabin so that the wind and air coming from the cave would blow through his room.

The patients were charged $8 per week for the

services.

Patients called their new home "Cave Village". To pass the long hours underground, they constructed new paths and even mapped unknown parts of the cave. Time was marked by the burning of tapers, hour by darkened hour. In addition to the candles, stearine, or lard oil, lanterns were used to light the cave. Patients ate their meals underground and menu offerings included deer and other game killed on the property. Many patients would also spend time trying to get plants to grow beside their cottages, a futile effort in the pitch black. On Sundays, the service of the Episcopal Church was read. Throughout it all, hope was high for a cure.

Conditions in the cave were harsh. Coughing from the constant smoke of the stoves grew worse. In addition, many of the patients complained of colds and cold-like symptoms. The high humidity of the caves caused the beds and clothing to dampen and mold and patients constantly had to dry their linens by hanging them over the fires, creating more smoke. Another doctor in the area, Dr. Charles Wright, wrote at the time, "Those patients who remained in the cave presented a frightening appearance. The face was entirely bloodless, eyes sunken, and pupils dilated to such a degree that the iris ceased to be visible, so that no matter what the original color of the eyes might have been, it soon appeared black."

Tourists were still going through the cave at the time of experiment and would pass by the huts.

Many would peek through the open doors of tents or peer into the windows of the TB victims. Some of the cave guides were also attendants and referred to the patients as skeletons.

The patients grew steadily worse, rather than

The tuberculosis victims are buried in unmarked graves in 'The Old Guides' Cemetery located on the Heritage Trail near the gift shop and hotel of Mammoth Cave.

better. They complained to Croghan of being irritated with the constant smoke from the stoves which began to accumulate in the cave and began calling their new home the 'smokehouse'. Croghan persuaded them to stay, convinced the idea would work, and moved some patients farther back into the cave in a desperate hope to heal them. He also advocated keeping the temperature in the cave as low as they could stand it. In a letter of the time, Thomas Knox, friend to Croghan, stated "Everybody saw and knew that they were tottering on the brink of the cave; and yet, such was their hope-a distinct and inseparable accompaniment of the disease-that they could not be persuaded to quit that purgatory. They even imagined they were improving, and insisted that they were stronger, when they could not drag their deaden limbs after them."

Croghan himself mentions the

**Stephen Bishop, John Croghan and The Old Guides' Cemetery**

**When Dr. John Croghan purchased the property of Mammoth Cave, he also acquired Stephen Bishop, a slave who created one of the first known maps of the interior of the cave. For many years, Bishop was the lead tour guide and explorer in the caves. Bishop was freed from his servitude more than seven years after Dr. Croghan died, in accordance with his will. Bishop died one year later from tuberculosis. He was 37 years old. Bishop, like many other guides, was buried in the 'Old Guides' Cemetery' and his tombstone can still be viewed today.**

smoke in his private letters, stating that when the temperatures from the outside and the inside are the same, then the deadly smoke begins to collect.

He insisted this was the cause for the poor results. Eventually some of the patients began to realize the truth and wanted to leave. Croghan again persuaded them to stay.

The experiment would be abandoned in January of 1843, less than 5 months after it opened. Three of the patients would die in the cave and most would die within three days to three weeks of leaving Mammoth Cave House.

The victims:
1. <u>Dr. William J. Mitchell</u> from Glasgow, KY was the first to enter the cave on May 23, 1842. He left the cave just one month later, June 25, 1842. Mitchell was one of only two patients in the experiment who experienced any recovery in his health. He was married in September of 1842 and Croghan states in his private letters that Mitchell was often seen about the countryside, riding a horse. His improvement was short lived, however, and he died in the winter of 1842.
2. <u>John Wesley Harper, Esquire</u> was from South Carolina and entered the cave on September 15, 1842. Harper lived 2000 feet deeper, or farther, in the cave than Mitchell, hoping the deeper air would be more pure. He died January 18, 1843 and was buried near the cave.
3. <u>Oliver Hazard Perry Anderson</u> entered the cave October 20, 1842. He left the cave on January 11, 1843. Anderson would be

the greatest success story. He lived longer than any of the other patients, dying at 31 years of age on May 17, 1845.

4. <u>Benjamin Mitchell</u> entered the cave on December 28, 1842. Possibly near death already, Mitchell would die January 7, 1843. His would be the shortest stay and the first documented death of the patients.

5. <u>Reverend Charles Marshall</u> of Oswego, NY brought his wife along with him and possibly their four-year old child. His wife was utterly dedicated to him, living full time in the cave and only going into the sunlight once per day for brief periods. Marshall's hut was the deepest, being more than a mile from the front entrance to the cave. He was buried near the cave.

6. <u>Oliver P. Blair</u> died March 2, 1843. Blair was buried near the cave.

7. <u>Joseph Khleber Miller</u> was born in Sumner County, Tennessee. He was possibly the youngest victim at only 24 years old. He was also accompanied by his wife, Mary "Mollie" Franklin Miller. In addition, Miller also brought a personal slave named Peter. Miller died April 4, 1843 and is buried in Gallatin, Tennessee.

8. <u>Anne Marie Rose Parson</u> was the only female tuberculosis patient. Parson, in her late 20's, was from Cincinnati and died shortly after the cave closed.

Dr. Croghan considered the experience to be a failure and decided that nothing could cure the disease, "We are pioneers under all the disadvantages of such and after generations will reap the benefit of our experiment as I have no

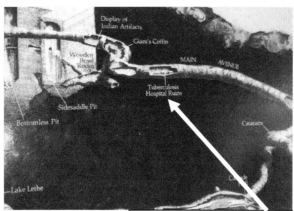

doubt this will divest the question of doubt and pave the way to improvements and its enjoyment under them by the afflicted world." Croghan held several theories as to how the experiment might have succeeded: if the sufferers could have stayed active and mined saltpeter, extended their stay longer or perhaps made daily trips into the fresh air above. He even considered having pure cave air piped into the buildings on the surface instead of having patients live

> Two of the original TB huts can still be seen on the Violet City Lantern Tour at Mammoth Cave. Only one is left standing and even that is in ruins. This sign outside the visitor center references the almost-forgotten tuberculosis hospital, the world's first devoted to a cure.

underground.

Dr. Croghan would not try a second experiment and returned to his ancestral home in Louisville. He would die from tuberculosis in 1849.

## Louisville's First Tuberculosis Hospital: Hazelwood Sanatorium

It soon became apparent that, unless something drastic occurred, tuberculosis might very well infect the entire city. Louisville's first attempt to stem the rising epidemic would be the creation of an open-air clinic. The State Tuberculosis Sanatorium opened its doors September 7, 1907. The small hospital was built on a hill just six miles from the downtown city on 52 acres. Nearby was a local rail stop, Hazelwood Station on the 17th street car line near what we today call Taylor Boulevard. In time, the name of the clinic would be changed to Hazelwood Sanatorium.

The clinic was quite small with a capacity for only ten beds. Soon, though, the hospital was filled to capacity. By 1910, the small clinic had grown to three open-air cottages-called "shacks", a sewage disposal plant, a dairy barn, a garden and several tents for the male patients. An average of 74 cases would be seen that year with the length of stay around 101 days.

In 1914, the facility had room for 60 beds and was often filled to capacity. In 1917, that number would grow to 140 with a waiting list and in 1919, over 145 were being admitted and treated. In 1920, the hospital was full with a waiting list of 20.

Patients would sleep in these open-air cottages year round, hoping to delay the effects of the disease.

Eventually Hazelwood would have to expand and another large, two-story building would be added with screened-in porches on all four sides. The hospital was the only one of its kind in the entire state, accepting tuberculosis victims from 115 Kentucky counties. Dr. AP Morgan Vance was hired to direct the sanatorium.

While the cost was free for the patients, each county was required to pay for the treatment. To gain admission into Hazelwood, each TB victim would have to apply to the fiscal court of his or her home county. The cost was up to $2.85 per day. A majority of fiscal courts around the state, already feeling the effects from what would soon be known as the Great Depression, refused to pay. When a patient account was delinquent for more than one month, they would be discharged from the hospital. One can only imagine what

A primitive solution for tuberculosis victims.

happened to those citizens who couldn't pay and couldn't care for themselves. While few counties had their own hospital, many did have "fresh air shacks" for the sufferers. Charitable donations were also made through local men's and women's clubs.

Money troubles plagued the public institution almost from the day one. The first announcement of hospital closure was made on August 1, 1914. Administrators insisted the high cost of maintenance, healthy food and quality care was very expensive and that the small average number of patients who could pay did not equal the expenditures. One solution to the financial troubles arrived in 1918 when it was speculated the War Department might take over the grounds for use as an army hospital. The board's hope was dashed, however, when the property was deemed too small for consumptive soldiers.

Finally, the State of Kentucky assumed ownership of the hospital in 1920. For a time, the hospital would also house World War I veterans along with consumptives. By 1924, the growing financial difficulties were becoming too burdensome for the state and patients were required to begin paying for their treatments. The weekly cost was $15 which was considered what each patient cost the hospital in treatment and food.

It wasn't long before the hospital was overcrowded and in disrepair. Newspaper reports at the time stated that the pipes in the old

> **In 1934, there were 12,456 confirmed TB cases in Jefferson County. Of those, 2,076 died, a ratio of one in every six persons.**

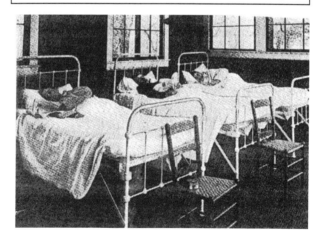

buildings were rusty, the lighting system was in dire need of repairs, the laundry machine frequently tore clothing, the refrigerators needed to be replaced and the shingle roof leaked often during rains. The outside fared little better. The walks on the ground were damaged and dangerous and the large herd of cows kept for fresh milk was costing more than what could be purchased from outside sources.

Dr. Paul A. Turner, superintendent and medical director spoke about the conditions in a news report, "The buildings and equipment at Hazelwood are in such poor condition that unless immediate repairs are made it will have to be closed. When it rains, attendants are kept busy moving patients from under the leaks in the roofs. The boilers in our heating plants have been condemned by a boiler expert, and we have been purchasing foods and medicine on credit that has been extended by Louisville business men. If Kentucky, which does less than any other State in curing tuberculosis, allows its only institution for that purpose to close, it will require twenty years to build back where we are today."

Closure of the facility, though, was not an option-not with so many dying from the disease. Also, Hazelwood handled all the surgeries for the state's other six tuberculosis hospitals and accepted patients from 26 counties. While Hazelwood would often struggle with funding issues, it would remain open and enhancements and additions over the years ensured that many lives were saved. Hazelwood operated at near-capacity throughout its history. Even in 1954- more than ten years after a cure for tuberculosis had been found-Hazelwood would have over 240 patients and a waiting list of 19. Although Waverly Hills would become more widely known, Hazelwood would remain open longer even accepting the last of Waverly's patients when the hospital was forced to close in 1961.

In 1970, the General Assembly transferred Hazelwood to the State of Kentucky and converted the hospital for the care of the severely retarded and mentally handicapped.

In the 1940's Hazelwood charged $2.85 per day for patients in advanced stages of tuberculosis. Only $1 per day was charged for all other cases.

# Chapter Four
# New Beginnings:
# The Creation of Waverly Hills

Perhaps the most famous of the tuberculosis hospitals in Kentucky was Waverly Hills Sanatorium in Louisville. The plot of land chosen for Waverly was far from the confines of the city, a remote ten miles from the center of downtown on a hill 300 feet above the Ohio River. The remote location, high altitude and county atmosphere were perfect for those suffering from the dreaded disease.

The area where Waverly now sits was simply farmland in those early days, far from the hustle and bustle of one of the nation's fastest growing cities. There were fewer than 120 families in the entire area. The only business was a dairy owned

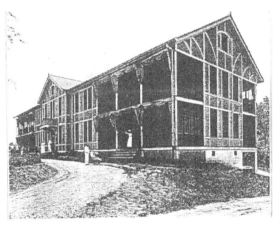

One of the earliest pictures of the original Waverly Hill Sanatorium.

by the Hettinger family, named Chesterfield Dairy. Many residents referred to the lands as Chesterfield Station, named for the rail lines that ran nearby and picked up milk from the dairy. Residents from the city referred to the area as 18th Street Road. Dixie Highway would not begin construction until 1915.

| Tuberculosis Statistics | | |
|---|---|---|
| Year | Number of deaths per 100,000 in Kentucky | Number of deaths per 100,00 in United States |
| 1907 | 225 | |
| 1910 | 242 | 160 |
| 1911 | 276 | 130 |
| 1921 | 177 | 114 |
| 1926 | 119 | |
| 1927 | 94 | |
| 1928 | 79.2 | |
| 1929 | 103.2 | 69 |
| 1930 | 105 | 97 |
| 1933 | 54 | 60 |
| 1934 | 90 | |
| 1935 | 66 | |
| 1936 | 74 | 56 |
| 1937 | 87 | 54 |
| 1938 | 75 | 49 |
| 1939 | 60 | 47 |
| 1940 | 64 | 46 |

It is from Major Hayes, and his daughters, that we have to thank for the picturesque name of Waverly Hills. When Major Hayes purchased the land, he had constructed a one-room schoolhouse off Pages Lane for his daughters' use. He hired Miss Lizzie Lee Harris as the teacher. The rolling hillside where the school sat reminded Miss Harris of a series of books popular at the time. The author of those books was Sir Walter Scott and they were called *The Waverley Novels* because the first book in the series is *Waverley, or 'Tis Sixty Years Since*. Other popular books in the series were *Rob Roy*, *Quentin Durward* and *Ivanhoe*. The books were popular because of their themes of tolerance regardless of class, religion, politics or ancestry as well as advocating social progress.

The Waverley School soon became known as Waverley Hill and that name was kept when the Board of Tuberculosis Hospital purchased the land although the spelling has since changed to 'Waverly'.

Waverley Hill Sanatorium was created in 1908 by an act of the General Assembly of the Kentucky Legislature. This act authorized all cities of the first class in Kentucky to form a ten-person board that would be known as the Board of Tuberculosis Hospital. The Board's main purpose was to erect and maintain a hospital specifically devoted to consumptive care. All members appointed to the Board would be assigned by the current mayor and would serve terms of four years without any monetary compensation. The Board's first meeting was held on January 4, 1907 where it was decided to levy a tax and accumulate all monies until such time as a hospital could be built. The first levy imposed by the Board was ½-cent on each $100 worth of taxable property for those living within Jefferson County. It would be two more years before enough revenue was created to finish the hospital at a cost of over $75,000 for the two-story wooden structure. The tax levy would increase yearly to accommodate the growing needs of the population and by 1920 was up to 6 cents, creating between $180,000-$200,000 revenue.

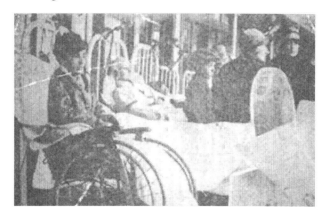

Waverly Hill, the first hospital of its kind, was designed by local architect James J. Gaffney who also designed the Southland Electrical Company Warehouse on East Jefferson Street and the Adath Jeshurum Temple and School on Brook Street. Waverly Hills opened its doors on July 26, 1910 to just eight patients, although the building could hold as many as forty. The original campus had just two buildings devoted to the care of the sick and one administration building. One building was reserved for advanced cases and one was for the treatment of those patients deemed curable. A news article at the time states only about 25% of patients were in the early stages and more than 50% in the advanced stages.

The Tuberculosis Dispensary, seen here in the background, was located at 121 West Chestnut Street in downtown Louisville.

Dr. A.M. Forster was hired as the Medical Director and Superintendent on January 1, 1910. His first act as Medical Director was to add eight more beds to the hospital which had been open less than six months and already running at full capacity. The formal dedication and opening ceremonies would be held on October 12 of that same year. When the city of Louisville decided to build a new City Hospital, an announcement was made that all tuberculosis patients would be moved to the sanatorium. Tuberculosis patients would no longer be welcome at the city's hospitals. Waverly would more than double its enrollment with the move which would cost another $25,000 just to deal with the more advanced cases.

| Year | Number of deaths per 100,000 in Kentucky | Number of deaths per 100,00 in United States |
|---|---|---|
| 1907 | 225 | |
| 1910 | 242 | 160 |
| 1911 | 276 | 130 |
| 1921 | 177 | 114 |
| 1926 | 119 | |
| 1927 | 94 | |
| 1928 | 79.2 | |
| 1929 | 103.2 | 69 |
| 1930 | 105 | 97 |
| 1933 | 54 | 60 |
| 1934 | 90 | |
| 1935 | 66 | |
| 1936 | 74 | 56 |
| 1937 | 87 | 54 |
| 1938 | 75 | 49 |
| 1939 | 60 | 47 |
| 1940 | 64 | 46 |

All patients, transferred in inter-urban freight cars, were moved to Waverly on August 22, 1911. Unfortunately, there was no room for them so they were forced to sleep in temporary quarters-canvas tents-until December 18, 1912-nearly a year and a half later. The $35,000 addition, $10,000 more than expected, for advanced tuberculosis patients allowed nearly 50 more consumptives to receive care.

The hospital on the hill wasn't the only method the city had to care for its tuberculosis patients, though. A downtown clinic, the Tuberculosis Dispensary, was in operation as early as June of 1907 with volunteer physicians giving treatment near the Louisville College of Pharmacy. Free examinations were given every morning from 9 until 11 o'clock for those unable to pay.

| Year | New Patient | Home Visits | Patient seen at Dispen-sary | Previous Patients Rein-stated |
|---|---|---|---|---|
| 1910 |  | 7600 | 815 |  |
| 1911 | 800 | 11,000 | 2400 | 143 |
| 1912 | 853 | 11,363 | 2450 | 205 |
| 1913 | 894 | 13,600 | 1550 | 142 |
| 1914 | 1250 | 21,000 | 2100 | 257 |
| Total | 3797 | 64,663 | 9315 | 747 |

Another major project of the Board of Tuberculosis was a training school and program for nurses. When Waverly Hospital opened its doors, the Tuberculosis Dispensary, through the use of only 7 nurses, was already caring for more than 400 patients in their homes. The nurses' main job at the dispensary was to make home visits. These visits were necessary for two reasons: to keep track of infection rates and to instruct caregivers on proper treatment methods. The nurses were also responsible for training family members in sanitary living conditions and some treatments were administered on an out-patient basis. Many patients refused treatment outright which made the job much more difficult. Many patients would arrive at Waverly only after careful screening and at suggestions of these nurses. Nurses being trained at the Dispensary were required to spend four months on home visits, twenty months at Waverly Hills and one full year in the Public Hospital. The nurses were paid $5 per month for the service of being of the front lines of the war against tuberculosis.

Tuberculosis was an epidemic nationwide with no end to the growing death toll in sight. Soon the tiny hospital had more patients than it could care for. Officials began making plans to accommodate more victims although there was no money for the project. The issue was quite controversial at the time even though there was considerable need for more beds. A bond was issued for the enhancements and presented to the public for a vote. Articles and advertisements littered the newspapers urging the citizens to approve the project.

| Year | Daily Average of Patients Admitted at Waverly Hills Tuberculosis Sanatorium |
|---|---|
| 1910 | 8 |
| 1911 | 61 |
| 1912 | 89 |
| 1913 | 110 |
| 1914 | 140 |
| 1915 | 170 |
| 1919 | 180 |
| 1922 | 200 |
| 1926 | 435, waiting list of 30 |
| 1930 | 450 |
| 1931 | 526, with 252 employees |
| 1932 | 480, waiting list of 75-100 applicants |
| 1933 | 488, waiting list of 150 |
| 1934 | 503 |
| 1935 | 515 |
| 1936 | 504 patients, 394 discharged |
| 1937 | 504 patients, 62% of patients discharged were either greatly improved or had their cases arrested completely |
| 1941 | 501 |
| 1943 | 497 |
| 1954 | 393 |
| 1956 | 346 |

In 1922, A.H. Bowman, president of the Jefferson County Board of Tuberculosis Hospital, officially announced Waverly Hospital was overcrowded with 200 patients in a building designed for only 40. The situation was critical. The building was referred to as a "fire trap" by the Louisville Courier-Journal and had been condemned by both building and fire officials. Speaking in an interview, Bowman said, "There is not room to isolate patients, and in fact the building is so crowded that we have no place for patients to die…..Patients are crowded together in an insanitary inhuman manner because of the lack of room. The negro ward is so congested that only the sexes are separated and children and adults are thrown together as is also the case with far advanced and incipient cases."

Bowman stated that were 2500 TB victims in the city and county that desperately needed hospitalized treatment but there was nowhere for them to go. They had to remain at home, infecting families, friends and neighbors who might come in contact with the disease, spreading it even more. Patients at the overcrowded hospital were forced to sleep on the open porches year round, in the severest of weather because no other beds could fit inside the building. Three physicians were on staff, dreadfully overworked

| Year | Population of Louisville |
|---|---|
| 1907 | 218,169 |
| 1910 | 223,928 |
| 1911 | 225,024 |

and possibly already infected. Fifty of those patients were children, some as young as eight months old.

B. Sanders, an employee of the hospital, agreed about the dire conditions inside the existing structure and stated to news reporters, "If a person in the last stages should suddenly collapse, the person next to him would have to lie there and see him die."

Bowman insisted the new hospital could prolong the lives of as many as 1300 residents and could cure the children presently infected in as little as six months. Dr. Brown, a doctor at the hospital, emphasized the urgent need to the public. "Tests have shown that by the time he or she reaches 30 years of age, every man and woman has the tubercle bacillus implanted in the body." Brown urged residents to protect their children by guarding their milk supplies and having yearly x-rays performed. The mayor of Louisville, Huston Quinn, agreed with Brown and was quoted in a newspaper as saying, "One in 12 of us here today is doomed to die. Statistics from the Health Department showed that one person out of every twelve is a victim of the disease."

Fortunately the public agreed and in 1923 approved the building enhancements at Waverly. The new building would house 435 beds and would open to a waiting list of thirty women. One year later, Waverly would have to expand again with an increase of 100 more beds. The hospital would also have quarters inside the main building for over 200 employees. With the increase, another 80 acres of land was added to be used for farming for the patients and staff.

Since Waverly was a county institution maintained by taxpayers, only residents of Jefferson County would be allowed on the waiting list. Residents outside of Louisville or the county would be declined admission and referred to nearby Hazelwood Hospital, an institution open to all residents of Kentucky. The new hospital was to be operated free of charge to the public with the city of Louisville and county of Jefferson jointly defraying the expenses. The City of Louisville would pay $750,000 and Jefferson County would pay $300,000.

This 1926 photo shows the original entrance to the hospital.

The architect of the new building was Arthur Loomis with DX Murphy and Brother serving as associate architect. Loomis also designed other well-known buildings in the area including the Carnegie Library in New Albany, Indiana, the Conrad-Caldwell House, a Victorian mansion in Old Louisville, and the Speed Museum on the University of Louisville campus. The hospital was patterned after a World War II Veteran Tuberculosis hospital in Dayton, Ohio. Three construction companies submitted bids for the project: Brashear and Cahill, CA Koerner and Company and Struck Construction, who placed the lowest of the bids and was awarded the contract.

Groundbreaking for the new Waverly Hill Tuberculosis Hospital took place on May 12, 1924. The event was planned with that date very specifically in mind. Special celebrations were to be held at every hospital in the city to commemorate the birth of Florence Nightingale in celebration of 'National Hospital Day'.

The celebration began promptly at 3 pm in the afternoon and included several notable Louisville residents. A.H. Bowman made an introductory address and L.D. Greene gave a speech entitled "What Our Hospital Means to Us". The Reverend Dr. Joseph O'Neil gave the invocation and Henry M. Shilling donated the service of his orchestra. For the patients who were unable to leave their beds, being entertained by the orchestra that day was one of their only pleasures. The hospital was opened to the general public and those attending were able to view special pathological exhibits, lantern slides, stereopticon views, and even exhibits in the X-ray laboratory.

The new structure cost approximately $3600 per bed and would be over two and a half years in the building. The new hospital opened to patients on October 17th, 1926 with dedicatory exercises on the following day. On October 18th, an open house was held at 3:15 in the afternoon following a luncheon at 12:15 at the Brown Hotel. Speaking that day, A.H. Bowman insisted that the new hospital was well worth the monies and efforts. "One out of every ten persons who died in Kentucky last year was a victim of TB. The new hospital will give the county one bed for every one of those deaths."

The wards in the hospital were composed of long hallways with rooms leading off on either side. The new five-story structure was considered one of the best hospitals in the country for treating TB and provided its patients the best therapy available at that time. Each room housed two patients and opened up onto a "sleeping porch" 600 feet long which faced the south side of the building, taking advantage of the afternoon sun. Each bed in the hospital was equipped with a radio, a telephone, a bell signal and an electric light socket. The new hospital boasted a kitchen, laundries, x-ray rooms, sunporches and parlours, a motion picture theatre, library, bakery, sterilization equipment and modern labs as well as being fire resistant, a unique concept in those days. Many public-minded and philanthropic citizens around Louisville helped with the effort and spent their private monies equipping rooms at a cost of over $500, quite a substantial amount in those days. One family, Theodore Ahrens and his daughter Mrs. Elsie Zinsmeister, donated monies to equip an entire ward.

> **Between 1904 and 1960, over $2 million would be collected from the bond. Of the city tax rate of $2.36 per each $100. 6 cents went to the sanatorium. The bond was not fully paid off until 1963.**

Surely, with so much help at hand, the rising death toll would be abated. For those living in Jefferson County, Waverly was their last hope at a cure.

There are several problems with obtaining accurate death counts from Waverly Hills. Originally, all deaths at the hospital would get tabulated as county deaths. Prior to the 1920's many of the deaths would be logged in the home addresses of the deceased and not at the place of death. Oscar O. Miller, administrator, said, "In the past, we have been unable to get a true picture of the TB situation in Louisville due to the method of keeping statistics." Although accurate death statistics are nearly impossible to get, there are some reports available which included the following information:

*One of the first statistics stated that 225 persons died at Waverly in 1907.

*542 died in 1910, one of the deadliest years.

*Waverly reported that 322 patients died in a four-year period beginning in 1911, at the rate of one patient every four and half days.

*170 would die in 1912 alone.

*The death rate would continue to rise and in 1921, there were 437 deaths.

*275 would die in 1923.

*In 1940, the death rate would begin to decrease and only 191 would die at Waverly.

*The 1950's saw the lowest deaths from TB: 80 persons in 1952, 66 in 1953 and 42 in 1954.

# Chapter Five
# Time Heals All Wounds:
# Life at Waverly Hills

The primary method of treatment at Waverly was simply bed rest. At that time, rest was the foundation for all tuberculosis treatments. A Louisville nurse said in an interview in the early 1900's that "an invalid must do nothing to create a fatigue that he may not overcome easily by a very reasonable amount of rest." Even after the initial fevers would pass and it appeared as if the patient were going to recover, he or she would still be required to remain in bed with a 'normal' temperature for several more months.

Patients at Waverly could be expected to spend several hours per day on the porches, or solariums. The original porches ran the length of the building and were not enclosed with glass. Screens were the only thing separating the patients from the weather and, even in freezing cold conditions, the patients would be wheeled out each day to partake of the fresh air. All patients who could stand the cold weather were expected to spend as much time as possible outside, some even sleeping there year-round. The open air porches also allowed fresh air to circulate throughout the hospital, expelling the germs that were sneezed or coughed out into the air. The patients were expected to be always in the open air, except for blowing rains or intense cold. In winter, they would be dressed warmly in flannel and wear toboggans, lying underneath many blankets. Fortunately electric blankets had very recently been invented and provided comfort to a great many. Each day, patients were given long rest breaks where they were not allowed any form of entertainment. They were not allowed to read or even talk; they could do nothing but sleep.

The building was designed in a curve, as seen here, to take full advantage of the breezes that would flow through the porches. That's also the reason the building was erected on top of the hill-to allow for natural air-conditioning from the breeze flow.

For those more industrious, walking exercises on the winding road of the campus also allowed TB patients to be out in the fresh air, expanding their lungs. Regardless of the quiet, restful condition, Waverly did provide some forms of entertainment for its patients. The Director of the hospital in the 1920's reported on the variety of activities in a Louisville Times news article, "'The institution furnishes suitable recreation and diversion for the patient," Dr. Oscar O. Miller said. 'There is a picture show every Wednesday night and prayer meetings, Sunday-school and church services. We have a department of

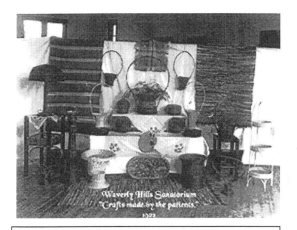

**Some of the items produced at Waverly would be displayed at the Kentucky State Fair. Waverly patients won prizes at the fair for three years straight. All profits generated would go back into improvements and operating costs for the hospital. Funds from the small store paid for such things as an elevator and even surgical supplies.**

occupational therapy where the patients do weaving, basketry, tool leather work, wood carving, needle work and many of the other arts and crafts. The radio-phones are so constructed that a programme may be radiocast from the sanatorium. We have a library, a beauty parlor and a well-equipped store.'" Drama clubs, singers, dancers and magic acts from Louisville also occasionally presented programs for the patients.

Occupational therapy allowed the residents the opportunity to do something positive and productive with their time. The patients were taught how to weave baskets and make items such as brooms, toys, tablecloths, bedspreads, baby clothes, hook rugs and other items. The occupational therapy room was also a gathering place for many residents who wanted to simply socialize, play cards and work puzzles-a get-away from the serious business of recuperation. At first, patients would only be allowed a few minutes of therapy per day. As their health improved, some patients would gradually work up to a full day's work on the property. Girls could be expected to learn needlework and embroidery and there was a workshop for the men. The Occupational Therapy shop would occasionally be opened to the public in open houses and items sold that were made by Waverly residents.

The occupational therapy teachers also made sure each resident learned a new trade so that they could have a livelihood when reentering society. In addition to crafts, students were also instructed in wood carving, toymaking, rug and mat weaving, leather cutting, copper hammering, bookbinding, dressmaking, and basketry.

Letter writing was another favorite occupation and enough mail was generated that a post office was designated at the hospital in April, 1931 changing the route from nearby Valley Station.

> Halloween has historically been a much celebrated event at Waverly Hills (evn today!) and yearly parties were given. In 1928, a popularity contest was held for "King of the Hill". All the candidates were radiocast and patients voted for their choice. Mr. Abe Netter, the favorite, was defeated by only one vote. The winner that year was James Abraham Lile. His queen was Miss Juanita Regina Powers. Other members of her court were Marty Lydon, Della Hill, and Marion Burkhart. The event was quite a gala with all queen candidates wearing gowns. The king and his queen were both crowned at the Halloween party which every patient attended, except those confined to strict bed rest who listened to the fun on a Waverly radiocast. To ensure the children didn't have too much fun, alternate party games were invented and played including making and decorating Halloween masks, word games, writing poetry and grabbing fortunes. In a sanitary twist on the traditional apple-bobbing, Waverly residents went 'marshmallow bobbing', a game where marshmallows were tied to a long string and the participant had to eat their way to the end first!

The Fourth-Class post office handled all mail and Waverly Hills Hospital became its own town, Waverly Hills, Kentucky.

Reading was another restful, but enjoyable, activity and Waverly had its own library run by local women's groups. The library had both books and magazines and reading materials would be delivered to the bedsides on a tea wagon. Patients would be given a choice of several books. Book and magazine drives were held quite often and the public was invited to participate. Local notices in the newspaper advertised the events but many of the books would simply be given by friends and family members when they visited.

Waverly also had an adult education program, run for many years by Esther Haskell and sponsored by the WPA (Works Progress Administration). Some classes would be taught in chart rooms, some on the solarium, some in the ward. For others, Ms. Haskell would conduct lessons at the bedsides. She taught everything from shorthand to Shakespearian drama.

There were many educational opportunities for adults at Waverly and most were prepared by Ms. Haskell herself. She would hand write the lessons, then mimeograph and give those to each of her 400 students. While her sickest pupils would rest each day from 1 to 3 pm, Ms. Haskell would give shorthand and typing lessons to the nurses. While patients could also take these types of lessons, it was only with the doctor's approval as they were more strenuous.

In addition to the adult classes, Ms. Haskell would also read the news and current events over the loudspeaker systems two mornings of each week. While the opportunity to learn was probably cherished, even an adult education teacher was still just a teacher. In a 1937 article, Ms. Haskell related a prank played on her by residents of the hospital. During her weekly news reading over the loudspeaker, Ms. Haskell was dismayed to find that one or more of her students had disconnected the plug and no one in the hospital had heard one word of her one-hour lecture. Not to be daunted, she simply plugged it back in and began again!

---

**Staff and Patient Waverly Publications**
- *Waverly Monthly*-published stories and poems written by residents, mostly the young women in the 5th floor Girls Ward.
- *Waverly Chronicle*
- *Bulletin*

---

There were many other teachers at Waverly, some of whom began as patients themselves and then wanted to give back to the institution that had healed them. Mrs. Ruth McFerran Leach was once such teacher in the 1940's and held commercial classes at the hospital four mornings a week. Leach instructed young women on typing, bookkeeping and shorthand in a job training program sponsored by the Women's Advisory Committee and the Jefferson County Board of

Education. Through the program, students were placed into jobs as soon as leaving the hospital.

Other training programs would exclusively train young women. Future housewives were taught how to save energy and time on household tasks while working women would receive employment training in fields chosen to account for their physical limitations.

Waverly residents recall other fond events such as the yearly visit from Santa Claus who would arrive on the front lawn with a sled and take all the children for a ride. Yearly Easter egg parties were held and children would roam the grounds to find the hidden eggs. Unauthorized nightly card games were also held and many residents remember sneaking down from their rooms to walk and socialize in the woods surrounding the hospital. A favorite activity of many patients was sneaking off the grounds of the hospital completely. A hamburger shop was located near the foot of the hill and many daring residents would leave through the tunnel and return with bags of hamburgers for their friends. Impromptu social gatherings were held in the rooms of the patients where some relate heating cans of food on the radiators and smoking with their friends, an activity allowed at Waverly Hills. There was also a kindly doctor on

> **Three transit lines operated between the city of Louisville and Waverly Hills: Louisville Railway Company, Greyhound Bus Lines and Fairdale Transit Company.**

the premises who would allow the children to take rides on his horse.

A beauty and barber shop was also made available to the resident twice weekly, one day for the men and one for women. Shampoos and waves cost 35 cents and children were treated for free. Church services were also held at Waverly weekly, one service for Protestants and one for Catholics and a chaplain was available for counseling and spiritual needs.

As the need for more beds increased and tuberculosis swept through the area, the hospital grew and expanded and a community developed. Most employees lived on the premises and received room and meals as partial work payment. For the employees who had close contact with the patients, going back into the public and possibly spreading the disease farther wasn't an option. Dormitories and wards were constructed as were large homes that several nurses shared. Many of the homes on East Pages Lane were originally constructed for the doctors and their families.

The hospital grounds grew much of their own food and at one time even raised hogs and cattle to provide meat and had a hennery for fresh eggs and chickens. The staff rarely needed to leave since they could order groceries from the storeroom and purchase other necessities at the hospital gift shop. However, a bus did make daily stops at Waverly and according to a 2004 article in The Louisville Courier Journal, "a former patient began making taxi runs".

The staff at Waverly Hills was an especially tight group. Many had left their homes and families to travel to the institution where they were quite literally sacrificing their lives daily to help the patients. Many nurses were once patients at Waverly who were so inspired they wanted to repay the debt done for them. Unfortunately, many dedicated nurses would also become patients as they contracted the disease.

Nurses weren't the only ones who sacrificed their lives. The doctors who worked at Waverly Hills lived on the grounds of the hospital in houses that can be still seen today on the road leading up to the hospital. The doctors would move their entire families into these houses and many of their children grew up on the hospital campus. Local residents also dedicated different services to the hospital, working to earn money at odd jobs such as working in the boiler rooms or on the grounds. Although risky, these jobs came at a time when money was scarce. Some would contract the disease.

For many, Waverly was simply home and while countless victims would unfortunately call Waverly their last resting place, a very great number of people found salvation at Waverly Hill and have many fond memories of their time there. Some residents, years later, would describe their fellow patients and even staff as family members.

| | Waverly Floor By Floor |
|---|---|
| 1st Floor | Lobby, Solarium, Patient Rooms, Offices, Medical Laboratories, Pharmacy, X-Ray, Dark Rooms, One Nurse's Station, Salon/Barber Shop, Dentist, Morgue (originally located at the foot of the hill), Kitchen, Food Coolers, Minor Surgery |
| 2nd Floor | Kitchen, Bakery, Dining Rooms, One Minor Surgery/Treatment Room, Solarium, Patient Rooms, Main Kitchen, Auditorium (for weekly picture show and guest speakers), Dining Room, Minor Surgery |
| 3rd Floor | One Surgery/Treatment Room, Solarium, Patient Rooms, Kitchenette, Dinette, Two Nurses' Stations, Kitchen, Minor Surgery |
| 4th Floor | Major Surgery Room, Recovery Room, Waiting Rooms, Major Surgery/Treatment Room, Solarium, Patient Rooms, Kitchenette, Kitchen |
| 5th Floor | Heliotherapy Department, Belltower, Children's Ward, Children's Play Area, Girls Ward for Young Women ages 14-25, Insane Ward (for those suffering from TB of the brain), Solarium |

Waverly Hills healing did not only exist at the hospital on the hill. Waverly, and the Board of Tuberculosis Hospital, had a huge outreach program, constantly trying to screen for new cases and educate the public.

One of the major focuses was on educating the next generation and the effort was poured into local schools. One program sponsored by the County Board of Education, the Lion's Club and the Tuberculosis Association was the creation of an open-air portable school. Camp Taylor Health School was created in 1926 and was the only one of its kind in the United States. Twenty of the most needy and underweight tubercular children in the county attended the school each day. Their ages ranged from 7 to 15-years old. Each day was filled with the same type of care that was given at Waverly: school work, special medical care, a diet that included morning and afternoon snacks as well as a heavy and hot lunch and then a special rest period. Since the school itself had no walls, in the coldest of weather, the children would have to wear Eskimo suits each day to school.

> A school puppet show in the 1930's was called "The Tubercle Tumbles" and featured four main characters: a little girl, Santa Claus, the Sun and a tubercle bug.

Funded primarily through the annual sales of Christmas Seals, yearly examinations were given at the Girls' High School in Louisville. This age group was in critical need since the TB death rate for women between the ages of 15 and 25 was nearly 75% higher than for the men of the same age bracket. In addition, the death rate among the women remained nearly level for over a decade in the 1920's while almost every other group was in decline.

Girls at the school would be examined once every year for their four years of high school. Louisville Girls' School was the first in the city and one of the first in the United States to annually scan young women in a public school setting. In addition to the medical examination, classes would be offered through the school on such topics as healthy grooming habits, keeping families healthy, and healthy nutrition. For those girls who were determined to be underweight, rest period were arranged during the school day and recommendations for treatment were given to their family doctors.

> **Open Window Week** was held each year at the beginning of November. The purpose was to acquaint citizens with the value of fresh air and encourage everyone to sleep with open windows during cold weather.

Health clubs were formed in schools around the county and the Tuberculosis Association would honor the local schools each year that had shown healthy attitudes and practices. Trophies, prizes and awards were given in ceremonies that honored the educational programs. In 1931, the Association even sponsored a "Health Pageant" with a fashion show that showcased young women carrying fresh vegetables, fruits and dairy. The winner of the pageant was determined to be the one "most healthy" and was given a crown. Children in all schools could look forward to the annual visit of the 'Health Gypsy' who educated the young about good eating habits and personal hygiene responsibility.

In addition to the tax levy, revenue was raised annually through the sales of Christmas Seals. It was a huge yearly event and nurses would circulate through the schools and libraries talking to the children about ways to keep disease free and eat healthy. Annual art shows were held and local schools did their part by giving a parade to raise awareness.

The annual 'Seal Sale' was a vital part of the huge effort to rid the city of disease. The seals helped to finance all local health examination clinics and in over six years in the 1930's, over 13,000 people were examined from as young as 2 weeks old to over 93. The monies from the sale also funded educational programs in public ad parochial schools as well as making possible examinations of industrial workers and paying for posters, leaflets, literature, radio talks, and

> In a 1931 newspaper article, Louisville Mayor William B. Harrison said, "We call upon our people, so blessed with good health, to purchase the little Christmas Seals offered for sale by the Louisville Tuberculosis Association. Not only do the little stamps add to the gaiety of packages and letters, but they have come to stand for the Christmas spirit itself-the old-fashioned, true Christmas spirit of doing something for those to who Santa Claus is but a lost illusion-to whom Christmas is but another day of pain."

billboards for public knowledge about ways to combat the disease. The seals also helped to create various health clinics around the city for both white and black citizens.

Approximately 45,000 letters would be mailed each year to the public as a reminder to participate. As many as 30,000 would contribute. The seals would be sold in a book for $2 and the booklet would contain 200 seals at a cost of 1 penny each. Local Girl Scout troops would help with the effort by folding thousands of booklets each year. The seals would be used to decorate Christmas letters and packages and became a tradition that still exists today. Boy Scout troops would aid in the campaign by making posters against public spitting and parading them through the streets.

Ads such as this were placed regularly in local newspapers reminding the public of healthy hygiene habits.

In its heyday the annual Seals Parade became an important Christmas tradition around the city. In addition to Santa and Christmas trees, local store window fronts would also display the characteristic double-barred cross, a symbol of The American Lung Association, then known as the National Tuberculosis Association. The Louisville Railway Company allowed the Tuberculosis Association to freely display placards on their street cars and to distribute advertising leaflets. In the 1930's local stores such as Baldwin Piano Company, Bankers Bond, Central Furniture, Consolidated Realty, Liberty Bank, Lincoln Bank, Rodes-Rapier and the Blue Boar Restaurant donated their storefronts to help with the annual push. One store on South Fourth Street

> The first Christmas Seals sold in Louisville were part of a public auction on November 28, 1908. $613 was raised among thirteen participants: FW Keisker, Bernard Bernheim, Henry Besten, John Smiley, WC Nones, IW Bernheim, WJ Abram, Rush Watkins, Bernard Flexner, Dr. CC Godshaw, Blakemore Sheeler, Washington Flexner and MJ Insull.

devoted its entire window to a physician and patient, showing the public the proper procedure for receiving a chest examination. Local movie trailers would also be run in area theatres.

Other local women's and men's clubs would regularly help with the cause. The second week of February was noted as "Tuberculosis Week" and local Elk lodges planned a tagged hunting day to celebrate. All monies raised were used for the first mobile tuberculosis clinic which took to the roads in 1942 and traveled all over the state.

As the disease death rates began to decline, the public would begin to lose interest in the cause. With the loss of interest came the loss of funding and volunteer efforts.

> **Although death statistics are nearly impossible to tabulate, the dispensary did report 891 known deaths in 1941 at one clinic alone. Tuberculosis would kill more than 4,000 in the years 1940-1941.**

Beginning in October of 1946, Waverly would begin asking patients to pay for the treatments on an ability-to-pay basis. Persons who were unable to pay had to be treated for free. The charges were $4 per day. Partial payment options were available. Patients were interviewed to determine their financial status and the information was verified through a local credit agency. Many patients would refuse to pay. Lawyers hired by the patients concurred that Waverly could not force some residents to pay and not others. Waverly would continue to operate free of charge.

Waverly's days were numbered. With little financial backing and the loss of public interest, politicians and civic-minded leaders began to consider the possibility of closing the doors on Waverly Hills Tuberculosis Sanatorium forever.

Letter to the Editor, Louisville Courier-Journal, December 7, 1927

"I am now and have been intermittently for over two years a patient at Waverly Hills Sanatorium, and as my life is now coming to a close, and may be by the time this reaches you, I feel not that I would have left something undone, if I did not while still conscious, express my deep appreciation to those who were the originators of the suggestion, as well as those who labored for the erection of this wonderful haven where the tubercular may have the very best possible care and treatment.

And I want to speak a word of appreciation and commendation for Dr. Oscar O. Miller and his splendid staff of physicians, the nurses and orderlies who have been not only patient and kind with me, but wonderfully sympathetic and responsive to my every need. Many of the patients, like myself, had nightmares before coming out here, fearful of what they were destined to go through, but after a day or two of residence, thanked God that there was such a place where either the incipient or the advance case would be given the most careful and sympathetic consideration. May God bless all those who are making this institution one of hope to those suffering from this dread disease, assuring them that over the door might be truthfully inscribed, 'he who enters here, may entertain hope of leaving cured, or much benefited', if the disease has not made too much headway."

-----Thomas Spies

## Chapter Six:
## Dying to Get Well
## Remedies, Cures and Treatments

Besides open air and bed rest, Waverly Hill did have other treatment options for patients and was considered to be one of the best hospitals in the nation for TB victims. Dr. Benjamin Goldberg, Medical Director of the Chicago Municipal Tuberculosis Sanatorium and Associate Professor of Medicine at the University of Illinois was quoted as saying Waverly was "unsurpassed by any hospital of its kind in the United States". While many of the treatment options listed below may seem cruel and pointless, remember that no medicines had yet been invented that could cure

A Louisville nurse at the time said that one important consideration for a TB patient was that he "....should chew his food well."

tuberculosis. Penicillin, the most basic of modern-day antibiotics, was not invented until 1928 and was not used nation-wide for several years later. For many, treatment at Waverly was their only hope.

- **Nutrition**

Proper nutrition was almost as important for a healthy body as proper bed rest. Every patient at Waverly was expected to eat well and to eat every meal. Unfortunately, one of the side effects of consumption is lack of an appetite so this form of treatment wasn't as easy as it sounded. Patients at Waverly could expect to eat at least three full meals per day with several in-between meal snacks. Protein, fresh fruits and vegetables and dairy were high on the list. Over 2000 meals were served each day from the Waverly kitchens and the hospital had huge food coolers to contain all the needed supplies.

> In 1942, the War Foods Administration gave 2 train carloads of food to local hospitals including Waverly. Local Tb victims enjoyed one load of potatoes, one of evaporated milk and a supply of fresh eggs.

- **Heliotherapy**

Heliotherapy, today called light therapy or phototherapy, was another non-invasive treatment and consisted of exposing the patient to light, via either natural sunlight or an ultra-violet sunlamp. Although today we slather on layers of sunscreen to protect us from harmful rays, the use of light to heal has been used for centuries. Sunlight has been proven to kill some forms of bacteria, reduce pain and improve circulation-all effects that would certainly help to heal TB. In addition, exposure to light also raises the levels of vitamin D in the body, an important element needed to fight off diseases.

Heliotherapy was not used regularly for all forms of tuberculosis, only for those individuals who suffered from the disease in their bones, joints, skin, and eyes. At Waverly, some forms of heliotherapy were given on the roof of the building, on the fifth floor. Heliotherapy was an especially important treatment option for children since no surgery had to take place. Young TB

Many pictures exist of the solarium but there were actually two other types of rooms on each floor with an inner hall separating them. The rooms adjoining the solarium were for patients who could benefit from the treatments and fresh air. The enclosed rooms facing the front, or south west side of the building was for patients using heliotherapy. Heliotherapy was continued for them through the use of sunlamps.

victims were kept outside, sparsely clad, as often as possible to take full advantage of the healing effects of the sun.

- **Heliotherapy from sunlamps**

Sunlamps were also used at Waverly in heliotherapy treatment rooms, the precursors of today's tanning beds. The sunlamps were often brought out onto the porches, or solariums, where the lamp would be attached to the headboards of the bed so that the patient could take full effect of the breezes and both natural and artificial light.

The lamp would be directed towards the part of the body affected by the disease, most often the lungs. Eyes were covered to protect them from the UV rays. Initial treatments would begin with just three minutes of light until the body became accustomed to the rays and then gradually increased until patients were sitting for thirty full minutes, the longest amount of exposure allowed.

One type of sunlamp used at Waverly was called an Alpine sunlamp and it was used most especially in treating bone and abdominal tuberculosis. For patients suffering from tuberculosis of the larynx, a special set of metal mirrors were used to reflect light. Intestinal tuberculosis was treated with ultra violet radiation through the use of mercury lamps.

Heliotherapy is still being used today to treat a variety of disorders including skin conditions such as acne, eczema and psoriasis and emotional disorders such as seasonal affective disorder (SAD) and depression.

- **Postural rest**

For most of us, rest doesn't seem like a form of treatment, but Waverly employed many varieties in the treatment of tuberculosis. Postural rest involved forcing the patient to lie on his or her infected side, thereby restricting the efforts of the lung on that side and allowing it to heal.

- **Shot Bag Method**

This treatment option was for patients who were unfortunate enough to have both lungs infected. In this therapy, a bag containing one pound of gunshot would be placed on the patient's collarbone. The amount of shot in the bag would be gradually increased by four to five ounces per week. Eventually the patient might be wearing up to five pounds on each infected lung. Sandbags were occasionally used as well. While this was most certainly uncomfortable, the result of restricted breathing and movement allowed the infected lungs a chance to heal rather than labor in deep breathing.

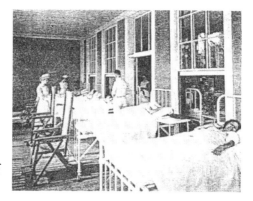

For many patients, however, more aggressive forms of treatment were needed and many desperate souls would travel from as far as 500 miles away to be treated at Waverly Sanatorium. Other curative options at Waverly focused on more aggressive treatments of the lungs. Fortunately, anesthesia was available and consisted of either nitrous oxide, also known as "laughing gas", ether, or occasionally cocaine.

- **<u>Cupping</u>**

Cupping was a process through which the source of consumption would be drawn out of the body. This would occur by first making an incision with a scalpel. Then, a preheated glass cup with rough edges would be applied to the open wound. As the cup and the air within it cooled and contracted, blood, tissue and pus would exit

> Early detection of TB was nearly impossible in the early 1800's. Doctors had little to go on until it was too late. The most telling sign, bright red foamy blood or sputum, often indicated a patient in the final stages. The stethoscope, a life-saving invention for many sufferers, was developed in 1816 by Rene Laennec, who needed an instrument to study the effects and diagnoses of many diseases. It was the first step towards diagnosing the quiet killer, the white plague. Laennec was perhaps motivated by the fact that his mother and dear cousin both died from tuberculosis. His own nephew used the invention to diagnose Rene's tuberculosis in 1862. He died just months later.

through the incision. While safe and not painful,

the treatment could leave the victims with temporary marking of the skin and there was a mild risk of burns.

This vacuum method has been around for centuries and is still commonly used in Greece, Russia, Mexico and China where it is helpful in treating colds, bronchitis and other respiratory illnesses.

> Waverly's state-of-the-art treatments were known nation-wide. In 1938 a movie was made about such treatments. Dr. H.E. Kleinschmidt, head of Health Education for the National Tuberculosis Association, produced a movie that focused on healing treatment options around the country. Waverly was chosen by the Association as one of the best hospitals in the South and one "eminently suitable as a model for all other sanatoriums". Photographs were taken in all parts of the hospital. Waverly was one of the first in the country to offer 'postural rest' treatments, where the patient would lie for an extended period of time with the feet elevated above the head. The movie was shown in theatres, schools, granges, civic clubs, colleges, medical associations and women's organizations around the country. The documentary was called "Tuberculosis in Retreat".

- **Pneumothorax**

Pneumothorax is a method of treatment where air or nitrogen was introduced into the pleural cavity of the lungs. To do this, a surgeon would use a needle to inject gas between the diseased lung and ribs. The infected lung would then be collapsed surgically, creating a pocket or cushion. This allowed the tissue and the lesions in the lungs to rest and heal without the pressure of using that lung for breathing. The treatment also reduced fever, cough, and expectoration and had a positive effect on appetite. (Balloons would sometimes be inserted into the lungs and then filled with air for the same effect-to provide relief to overworked, diseased lungs.) The collapsed lung would then return to its normal size in a few days.

Pneumothorax was considered a minor operation and could be performed at a patient's bedside. Only a local anesthetic, Novocain,

> **Patients undergoing the treatment commonly referred to it as "pneumo" or the "shot".**

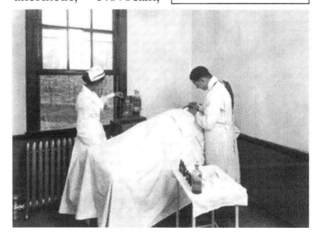

was needed and the procedure caused little discomfort, most often a shortness of breath. Pneumothorax treatments were given twice a week initially and then monthly and many patients would return for the treatment even when released from Waverly Hills. Some patients might get up to thirty "refills" a year! For many TB sufferers the procedure also allowed treatment without checking into the hospital as they could be treated on an 'out-patient' basis.

This procedure was very common in the 1920's and 30's across the United States. By 1937, it was estimated that between 50-80% of all tuberculosis patients were undergoing the treatment. The treatment most helped moderately advanced

> **What Could Go Wrong?**
> While pneumothorax was relatively painless, many patients did experience some discomfort and fatigue. However, for some, there were more serious side effects. A needle breaking off between the ribs was quite common as was perforations of lungs, stomachs, hearts and livers. If a doctor accidentally punctured a pulmonary vein, it could create an air embolism causing convulsions and even sudden death. Some patients had adverse reactions to the procedure and experienced terrible pain, fever and even hallucinations. While air was most commonly used to fill the lung cavity, there were reports of other substances being used including oleothorax (oil), gauze, paraffin, fat, rubber sheeting, bags and even ping-pong balls! This type of procedure was known as plombage.

patients who had not responded well to other non-invasive methods such as rest or heliotherapy. For patients in advanced stages with many lesions, the procedure was not possible.

Waverly patients taking their daily constitution-a walk around the grounds. It wasn't the exercise that was so beneficial, but the fresh air.

- **Avulsion/Phrenicotomy/Phrenic Nerve Crush**

Avulsion was one type of invasive surgery performed at Waverly. This procedure was known by a variety of names and was a nerve operation where doctors would remove or paralyze the phrenic nerve. This nerve causes the diaphragm to function and, when removed, paralyzed the muscle and allowed the lung to rest. In a phrenic nerve crush, the nerve would be paralyzed for a temporary period, usually between three to six months. Normal movement of the diaphragm would gradually return on its own. In avulsion, or phrenicotomy, the nerve would actually be severed. This caused a permanent paralysis of the diaphragm yet patients could still breathe, although breathing was labored. In some permanent cases, the surgery could be reversed if scar tissue had not formed.

While a popular procedure in its day, this surgery was not performed widely after the late 1930's. This procedure is occasionally still used to treat spinal cord injuries.

> **Ancient Cures**
> While such cures may seem odd to us today, it was certainly better than the treatments available in ancient Rome. Physicians there would routinely advise their TB patients to bathe in a healthy person's urine, eat the livers of wolves or drink the blood from an elephant!

- **Pleurectomy/Lobectomy**

Pleurectomy was a major surgery and involved removing part of the diseased lung. For advanced cases, the lining of the lungs could be removed as well as the chest wall and diaphragm. A lobectomy involved removing lobes of tissues of the lungs. This type of surgery was done to decrease the amount of pain a patient was in.

This procedure is still performed today for those suffering from lung cancer.

- **Pneumonectomy**

This was one of the most serious procedures and one of the last resorts. During pneumonectomies, an entire lung would be removed. This procedure was only performed when the diseased lung was beyond repair.

This procedure is still performed today for those suffering from lung cancer or other diseases involving the lung such as emphysema.

> **Just a Bad Day?**
> On Tuesday, December 19, 1950, a power outage struck Waverly Hills during a major operation. Normally stand-by batteries would be used but these, too, failed and the operating room was plunged into blackness. Batteries had to be taken from automobiles on the grounds so that surgeons could finish the operation. The cause of the black-out? Someone had fired a bullet into a local transformer.

- **Thoracoplasty**

One of the last resorts for tuberculosis patients was thoracoplasty. This was the most invasive and serious procedure performed at Waverly. During the procedure, the chest would be cut open and two to three ribs removed. Some patients would have to undergo the operation several times, removing as many as nine ribs.

This was done to create a huge air cushion in the lungs, allowing the chest wall to collapse in on itself. There was less room for the diseased lung to expand,

> In 1941, more than 900 people would be treated at Waverly Hills. 105 major operations took place that year as well as 108 minor operations.

forcing it to rest. This operation was permanent and the lung would not re-inflate as was the case during the pneumothorax treatment.

Although the patient was under anesthesia, it was considered a painful operation and was used only as a last resort. Only 5% of the patients who undertook the surgery survived. Most who survived were left terribly disfigured and in pain. Many patients, when released, would not leave their homes because of their appearance. For some, even this drastic procedure was not enough to cure the disease. For the most serious of cases, a portion of the diseased lung or the entire lung would be removed.

> **Tuberculosis Fast Facts**
> - ☑ In its early days, tuberculosis was nearly impossible to diagnose because the symptoms so closely resembled other killers of the day: bronchitis, typhoid fever, lung fever, sinusitis, pleurisy, emphysema, flu and even adenoid infection.
> - ☑ Some patients would expectorate (cough up) their own weight in pus in just a few weeks.
> - ☑ Tuberculosis can infect almost every kind of animal, including goldfish.
> - ☑ There are rumors that the coolers at Waverly were also used as morgues during the height of the epidemic.
> - ☑ 17% of all bodies at Waverly had to undergo an autopsy so that the hospital could keep their license.

Thoracoplasty is still used as a treatment for tuberculosis in developing nations and here in the United States for treatment of severe scoliosis.

The cutting edge treatment at Waverly soon became known all over the nation and many people from other sections of the state and southern Indiana would move to Louisville, desperately trying to establish citizenship for the sole purpose of being admitted to the institution. Soon, officials at the hospital would limit admission only to life-long residents of Jefferson County. Even then, there was a long waiting list of sufferers.

> While today's medical costs are sky-high for even the smallest procedure, that was not the case less than 75 years ago. In 1934, the total salary expenditure at Waverly was $187,772.42. The total cost of all supplies for that same year was $215.717.17. Waverly usually reported a surplus on their budget, even during the years of the Great Depression.

Many victims were doing whatever was necessary to gain admittance and Waverly officials soon had to conduct an exhaustive investigation of all new patients to ensure they were indeed lifetime residents of Jefferson County before they could even be placed on the waiting list. If a deception was discovered, the hospital had no choice but to remove patients from other counties, regardless of the severity of their disease. During one year, there were applicants from over 22 states and 63 counties in Kentucky. All would be denied admittance.

AH Bowman went so far as to mail notices to all County Judges and other interested officials in the state stating that the law prohibited Waverly Hills from treating any patient not from Jefferson County. Bowman stated that as many as 20 tuberculosis victims arrived each month, hoping for admittance.

> **A Snapshot, 1954**
> **Waverly had:**
> * 393 patients who stay an average of 373 days
> * 323 surgical operations
> * 28,000 vials of streptomycin, 2.5 million tablets of PAS, 144,000 capsules of INH
> * 65 nurses on duty
> * 3,168 books and 5,700 magazines in circulation
> * 1,147 barrels of milk
> * 13 tons of sugar
> * 6 tons of butter
> * 553 acres
> * 5,332 tons of coal which would take nearly one mile of coal cars to haul it all.

For those patients lucky enough to be admitted, the road to recovery was a long one. The average length of stay for tuberculosis patients at Waverly was 444 days, well over a year. One reason for this extended stay was due to the surgical procedures each patient had to undergo. Surgery was not done on patients immediately as many of them were in poor health, too weak to survive the surgical treatments. First patients would have to regain their strength and put on some weight before they were considered for surgery. While most patients needed only two operations, some of those in more dire situations might require as many as five! Patients would not be discharged until at least nine months after the surgical treatment.

Outpatient treatment services would not begin until 1956. In that year, 30 patients took advantage of the service and were allowed to take their medications at home. A check-up was recommended monthly and a chest exam and X-ray exam every three months. Only patients who were not at risk for infection were allowed to use the out-patient program. Some of them had patients at Waverly as long as four years.

How many would be saved by the radical medical procedures is anybody's guess. There are varying estimates of the death rates with many websites listing the total of deaths at over 63,000. However, that number is either an exaggeration or might point to the number of dead for the entire state or the county. Waverly Hills Tuberculosis Sanatorium was never meant to be a hospital for the dying. Many people, some still alive today, have these life-saving techniques and the dedication of the staff to thank for their long lives and ultimate triumph over the white plague, tuberculosis.

### Other Instruments/Treatments Used to Treat Tuberculosis

- Spirometer-This instrument, invented in 1846, was one of the first devices used for testing of tuberculosis in patients. It measured the amount of air expelled from the lungs.
- Medicated air aspiration-This device forced air into the lungs in order to overinflate them. They were also used to remove mucus and pus.
- Pneumatic cabinets-For this treatment, the patients would sit in an airtight chamber and breath medicated air through a tube. A common medicine at the time was creosote which was abandoned in 1900 as the drug was found to destroy the pancreas. This method was also referred to as a vapor bath.
- Bergeon Method-This treatment consisted of a rectal injection of sulfur dioxide. The patient would receive a mineral water enema straight into the intestines where the medication could be absorbed. This was abandoned in the 1900's.
- Vevesection-Similar to the above method except the medication and fluid was injected directly into the chest cavity.
- Electric therapy-For this treatment, a patient would grasp or step on a low-dose electric pole. Some patients would even inhale electrically charged gas. The theory was that the electricity would cause diseases to pass out of the body.
- Thoracentesis-In this procedure, a hollow needle is inserted into the lungs and used to draw out pus and other fluid accumulations.

# Chapter Seven
# The End of an Era:
# An End of the Tuberculosis Epidemic

Nationwide, the TB contagion at last seemed contained. Death rates were declining and the public was able to breathe a sigh of relief and concentrate on treating the last victims.

Unfortunately, that respite was to be short-lived. The 1930's were not kind to much of the nation and Louisville was no exception. A terrible drought swept through the rural, farming communities of Kentucky and the Great Depression began in earnest.

The city skyline before the flood.

Then, disaster struck. In January of 1937, the Ohio River Valley was inundated with over 15 inches of rain in just twelve days. The river flooded its banks, rushing through the streets and flooding over 70% of the city. It was quite possibly the worst flood ever in the state. 175,000 people were forced to leave their homes and many would remain homeless after the waters receded. With the waters came a higher incidence of disease of all kinds and tuberculosis would gain a new foothold in a city crippled by this natural disaster

Louisville would top the nation's list for highest number of tuberculosis-related deaths yet again. As money became more scarce and the city struggled to rebuild, public officials began looking for ways to cut budgets and scale back on unnecessary projects. Somehow, Waverly Hills Tuberculosis Sanatorium fell into that category.

One idea that was proposed to save money was consolidating all the local hospitals and placing them under a central administration. The proposal soon caught on and public officials called for Waverly Hills to be placed under the jurisdiction of the Health Department. For the first time in its history, Waverly was being asked to become dependent and relinquish control of patient care and funding.

Proponents began to see Waverly as an unnecessary and costly expense. The lack of centralized control and questionable admission policies topped the list of concerns. When funding was cut again in 1942, public and political officials began to act on the idea. A merger was proposed that would replace the board of directors, largely composed of private citizens, with city and county officials. Under the City-County Health Board Bill, all public health-related issues would be placed under the control of the mayor, county judge and three men who would be appointed by the State Board of Health. Under this bill, all monies would be put into a central fund. Money would no longer come straight into Waverly accounts. Indeed, under the proposal, not one penny of the funding would have to be spent on tuberculosis prevention or treatment. The bill was introduced by Senator Stanley Mayer, a Jefferson County Democrat. It was instantly met with controversy.

> **A Civic Duty**
> Waverly Hills would regularly x-ray and examine important community members such as teachers, janitors, food handlers, clerks, and bus drivers in all public and parochial schools in both the city and country. These jobs often dealt with the largest segment of the population and were the ones most likely to contract the disease. In 1941, Waverly would give over 7700 x-rays and was one of the first in the country to offer x-rays to teachers. Waverly also x-rayed all nurses in the health department, all pregnant women who came through the health department for care and all freshman medical students.

Two of the biggest adversaries in the very public fight were Edward H. Hilliard, Waverly Board member and Dr. Hugh Leavell, City Health Director.

Dr. Leavell argued that tuberculosis, while once an epidemic, was now declining in almost every state....except Kentucky. His suggestion was that Waverly was not as effective as other programs in other states. He also pointed that while the death rate was on the rise, it no longer claimed as large a part of the population, killing only 4% per year. He urged the citizens to consider the other 96% and their health needs.

Edward Hilliard felt that relinquishing control of tuberculosis care would mean a decrease in the amount of funding Waverly received and would cause a decrease in the care and treatment Waverly provided. Hilliard took out full page ads in the local paper reading "Help Save Waverly" and asked for the public to sign a petition stopping the bill. The editorial section was filled with doctors, patients, and recovered tuberculars extolling the care they received at Waverly and begging the public to stop the merger.

On January 26, 1942, a radio debate was held on WAVE. Dr. Leavell and Edward H. Hilliard hotly debated the issue. Leavell argued that the merger would reduce expenses, eliminate duplicate examinations and raise the standard of care the patients received, not just at Waverly but all over the city. Leavell also hinted that the doctors at Waverly were only opposing the move because they had been promised new equipment if the merger did not go through. Leavell also pointed out the rising healthcare costs associated with long-term tuberculosis care and was concerned about dwindling tax monies. Leavell stated that Waverly had never won a tuberculosis health contest, while both city and county hospitals had received awards for their work.

Hilliard continued to insist that money was the only reason for the merger. He felt the patients and their needs weren't being addressed.

The radio debate raised some interesting questions and an expert was hired by the mayor to end the dispute. David L. Robinson, a Public Administration Service employee from another state, spent 48 hours touring Waverly Hills. He was paid $250 and determined that Waverly Hills no longer helped tuberculosis patients recover.

Mayor Wilson Wyatt took the report into account and supported the merger. On January 29, 1942, by votes of 23 to 13 and 23 to 12, the senate included Waverly in the Health Bill merger. Waverly Hills, as a separate institution, ceased to exist.

Seven of the ten board members would resign in protest. Board members felt the move would decrease the standard of patient care and treatment and lower the level of disease management. The board members also feared the majority of funding would go to the Health Department, whose main concern was not TB, but general welfare of the population. Those who resigned included: A.H. Bowman, Robert T. Burke, Davis W. Edward, Edward H. Hilliard, Joseph T. O'Neal, W.S. Campbell, Dr. George S. Coon and Dr. O.O. Miller, who had served on the Board for 24 years. Only 3 remained: William Morrow, William Stoll, and William Day. Although Dr. Oscar Miller resigned, he agreed to stay with Waverly Hills on a temporary basis to ensure a smooth transition. He officially resigned a few months later, in July of 1942.

In 1943, Waverly Hills Tuberculosis Hospital merged with the City and County Health Department through Senate Bill 35.

One of the mayor's first acts after the merger would be to appoint Dr. Hugh Leavell as Director of the newly formed health board.

Shortly after the merger, vaccine for tuberculosis would finally be discovered and used for the general population. Tuberculosis death and infection rates would slowly begin to decline, although Kentucky would not see the same results other parts of the country were experiencing.

Waverly Hills continued to be plagued by bad press and bad luck. In 1945, a Republican County Commissioner, E.P. White alleged that the staff at Waverly Hills were conducting various illegal and unethical activities. White's major complaint was that Waverly officials had unfair hiring practices which caused a colleague of White's to not secure a contract with Waverly.

White also alleged that these same officials used politics in their hiring practices and even went so far as to shuttle patients to vote for Democratic political candidates in official Waverly vehicles.

White was not satisfied with the official

Churchill Downs, circa 1901.

response from administrators and next accused the staff of running an illegal gambling operation. Apparently, handbooks were being used by the patients to bet on the horses at Churchill Downs.

Waverly Hills administrators denied all wrong-doing but conducted an investigation in-house and submitted a report to White. White wanted more proof and asked the Fiscal Court to appoint the Jefferson County Medical Society to make an investigation. He felt the previously submitted report was not impartial because it was prepared by hospital administrators. He stated the public was demanding an explanation and urging for a new report.

The Fiscal Court voted 2-1 to begin a probe at Waverly Hills.

Waverly was inspected and a new report submitted to the court. The report showed White's allegation were mostly incorrect. The probe committee could find no evidence of favoritism or drunkenness on the part of any staff or employee.

The probe did find evidence of handbooking, however. Further investigation revealed part-time orderly Louis Stone did run such an operation. Sheets had been distributed with horses' names, jockeys, and the times of races and patients placed the bets from their bed. The race results were played over the radio except when it was the daily rest period, from 1-3 pm, and then the results had to be phoned in. Payouts were handled the next morning. Patients used the handbooks to wager on local horse races. Bets on the races varied from 10 cents to $1. Many felt this was not so much a gambling operation as simply a way to alleviate the boredom of patients confined to their bed all day.

> A new radio system was installed at Waverly in 1957. The new system allowed patients to hear one to three different stations through a pillow receiver attached to their beds. Previously, the radio system was limited to a single station played through individual earphones and the station was selected by one patient operation the master control in the main office.

In a Courier-Journal article at the time, an ex-employee and doctor who wished to remain anonymous commented, "Up to 10 cents, I would say betting is beneficial for patients." Stone agreed to stop the handbook operation.

The probe investigation did reveal some corrections: all general maintenance issues involving broken-down or old equipment that needed to be replaced

Waverly would apply for, and receive a $90,000 Federal grant and would use the monies to install elevators, reconstruct the refrigerated rooms and build staff rooms and offices.

Shortly after, in 1946, funding cuts began to seriously affect all county hospitals. Waverly was forced to cut 100 beds and decrease the number of patients being treated. That same year, Waverly would set records for the most visits ever with 5,854 in the month of May and set a record for the number of exams given at 3,784.

In 1954, ten years after the cure was discovered, almost 100,000 people in the United States would be diagnosed with the disease and 17,000 would die. Kentucky led the US states for highest death rate at that time. In Louisville alone, there were 7000 known cases and as many as 5000 not yet diagnosed. 104 would die that year. The State, desperate to halt the disease, would pass a law in 1953 that provided a jail sentence for any tuberculosis patients who

refused to cooperate with physicians or TB hospitals by refusing treatment and becoming a public hazard. Unfortunately, county jails had no facilities for treating TB prisoners so they were simply placed on probation then sent to a TB hospital. The hospitals, though, had no jurisdiction and could not imprison the patients. Many simply left when they wanted, venturing out into the public and infecting more of the population

These years were ones of explosive growth in the Dixie Highway area and what was once a peaceful farm community was being turned into a major development project. The area around Waverly saw the highest population and building growth during the 1950's, expanding more than 25%. Patients who had once come to Waverly for the clean air now had to be content with sulphuric acid, dust, smoke, ash, fumes and gases from various 'Rubbertown' industrial plants.

With the declining death rate across the nation came an end for the need for tuberculosis sanatoriums. The public, concerned with the Cold War, threats of communism and nuclear attacks and rising racial tension, seemed to feel that tuberculosis wasn't a concern. In 1954, almost 31 sanatoriums would be closed across the nation. Waverly Hills, an institution that had saved the lives of tens of thousands of people, was also becoming a thing of the past.

The State began giving aid to hospitals across Kentucky in 1952. The funds for Waverly continued to decline. In 1954, Waverly received only $200,000 almost half the amount allowed. The Health Board began to see Waverly as a huge drain on already tight city and county budgets. The other tuberculosis hospitals in the state were being financed completely through the state budget; why not Waverly? Many public officials felt that tuberculosis care was the responsibility of the state, not local governments. Besides, they argued, it was uneconomical to run two tuberculosis hospitals in the same county: Waverly and Hazelwood.

Public officials called for solutions to the financial crisis. Selling Waverly topped the list. An investigation into the matter found that Waverly, through excellent financial management, cared for patients at only $2.04 a day per patient. Other hospitals in the state nearly tripled that amount. Although a movement was made to close Hazelwood, the momentum was already too strong.

> ### A Cure At Last
> In the early 1940's, Dr. Selman Waksman, a Ukranian laboratory researcher at Rutgers University and Albert Schatz, a graduate student, discovered the cure for tuberculosis by accident. A farmer in New Jersey near the college informed Waksman that one of his chickens had become ill after pecking at some mold. Waksman wondered if this mold could be related to the same type of mold that produced penicillin, the current wonder drug discovered in 1928. The mold he found was not related to penicillin but was an antibacterial agent that could be effective, when combined with other drugs, against tuberculosis. The drug was soon being produced in 15,000 gallon drums and transmitted across the country. This triple threat-streptomycin, para-aminosalicylic acid (PAS) and isoniazid (INH)-soon halted the white plague. While there were some mild side effects and not all strains of TB could be cured this way, the reign of consumption was finally ended. Waksman was honored with the Nobel Prize in 1952 for his discovery. The first Tb vaccines were given in Chicago in May, 1942. Waverly would use the drug until 1948 when dihydrostreptomyecin would be discovered. The new drug produced less nerve damage and could be given in larger doses over a longer time period.

In 1960, only 270 patients remained in a hospital built, equipped and maintained for twice that amount.

The decision was made to close Waverly Hills Tuberculosis Hospital.

Waverly was to become vacant on July 1, 1961 but was able to close one month early. At the time of its closure, Waverly Hills included more than 553 acres and still had 120 patients. These patients would be transferred to newly-renovated Hazelwood Sanatorium, which was running close to pre-cure capacity at 307-occupied beds. The last tuberculosis patients left Waverly Hills on June 1, 1961, transferred by ambulance. Only a skeleton crew of maintenance and security guards were left and the gates were locked officially on June 15. On July 1, 1961, all patients became the responsibility of the state of Kentucky, not of Jefferson County, a momentous decision 50 years in the making. While the opening of Waverly was a ceremonial occasion attended by the community's brightest stars, the closing was of little fanfare and barely made a blurb in the newspaper.

## Crime at Waverly Hills

- In 1949, a twelve-year old patient informed the Juvenile Court Probation Department that she was two months pregnant. The father was a 21-year old intern in the Negro Division. A warrant was issued for Clarence Peasant of Louisville charging him with Carnal Knowledge. The young girl had only been a patient for seven months.

- Two criminals were captured in an unusual way at Waverly in 1945. Apparently, workers found former employee Elijah Butler, 39, asleep in the storeroom at the hospital. Upon investigation, workers found several items missing and another former employee William Thompson, 33, was implicated. Upon searching Thompson's home, police found 200 pound of sugar, two dozen quarts of vinegar and 50 pounds of coffee. Both men were charged with Grand Larceny and Storehouse Breaking.

- Mary Evelyn Vogler, 47, was struck and killed by a car driven by 24-year old Private Harold Sickles of Fort Knox, Kentucky. A $50,000 wrongful-death damage suit was filed against Sickles by Vogler's estate. Vogler was a nurse at the Waverly Hills and was crossing the highway in front of the hospital.

- In 1963, a 100-acre fire at Waverly Hills burned for several days before firefighters from five different firehouses were able to put it out. Police suspected arson.

## Chapter Eight
## A White Elephant:
## Life After Waverly Hills

Waverly Hills was for sale.

The building became little more than a white elephant for the county after closing its doors and the property was costing taxpayers between $50,000-$70,000 a year just in maintenance. Dr. Stuart Graves, Jr., Head of the Health and Welfare Council of Waverly Hills Committee, said, "The great problem we have is that the thing is so cockeyed big we can't get rid of it."

Board officials had the buildings and equipment appraised for $4.35 million. In addition to the main hospital, there were also 21 other buildings on the grounds. The value of the land was between $1500-$3000 an acre. The main hospital itself appraised for $1.5 million.

The first organization to express an interest was the Kentucky Methodists who made a formal announcement December 11, 1960, even before Waverly officials closed its doors. They were interested in the hospital as a home for the aged. The Methodists hired Harold K. Wright, Director of Institutional Services at a Chicago hospital, as consultant for the project. He toured the property in late December and informed the committee that major alterations would have to be made.

Another interested party was the City County Department of Health, who actually owned the lands and wanted to make a park of 273 acres. The park was to include a lake (by blocking off Bee Stream), a golf course, bridle trails and a forest. It was the only place for a park in southwestern Jefferson County. Charlie Vettiner, Superintendent of the Jefferson County Parks and Recreation, was a major backer of the idea but other members of the Health Department had wanted a quick and easy sale, hoping to get enough money to build a new health department downtown. The Health Department had already divided up the land for potential future use: save 14 acres for freeway usage; 12 acres for highway usage; 31 acres to the Illinois Central Railroad; 14 acres for a future expressway; 12 acres off Pages lane for residential use and keep 142 around the hospital.

On January 7th, Methodist Executive Secretary Dr. Walter Russell officially withdrew interest for his organization stating that the cost of remodeling the project, over $1.5 million, was too problematic.

On January 12, Kentucky Governor Bert Combs initiated another proposal- convert the property into a home for mentally retarded juvenile delinquents. Vettiner originally opposed the idea but later recanted, stating he supported any work done to help this needy segment of the population find a home. The hope was that federal monies would be available to help with the renovation and maintenance expenses. The City set the price at $1 million for the property. It would take another $3 million for renovation costs.

On a national front, this idea had important supporters. In October 1960, President Kennedy called for a national plan for dealing with mental retardation. In newspapers of the time, Kennedy felt the

> **Two Unique Proposals for the Waverly Property**
> 1. It was originally considered as a spot for the Louisville Zoo. However, it was located too far from the city.
> 2. A penal farm idea was proposed where county prisoners would farm, garden and tend animals. This idea was rejected due to security risks.

topic was the "most important and most neglected health problem". In 1960, over 5 million people suffered from mental retardation. In addition, the state of Kentucky was in a real crisis. The only location for dealing with the mentally retarded was the State Training Home for Retarded Children in Frankfort. Over 29% of the children at the home were from Jefferson County. There were 9000 mentally retarded children in the state and the average waiting time for placement was over six years.

After considering the costs involved, the plan was officially turned down by Governor Combs and the State Commissioner of Mental Health, Dr. Harold McPheeters on February 9, 1962. McPheeters said Waverly was not suited for children and was just a "big barn". He said $5 million in renovations were needed at Waverly and it wasn't suited for the needs of the children. There was a lack of adequate physical facilities, a lack of parking space and lack of heating since Waverly had always been an open-air institution. McPheeters said it would cost over $1 million a year to operate.

State legislators toured the building on February 14 and felt the building was in good shape and should be utilized by the state. They reported that if the rooms were enlarged the property could house over 500 beds. Some other positive features were an auditorium, a newly equipped operating room, an ice making machine, and a refrigerated garbage storage. After the tour, the price on Waverly was reduced.

Combs himself would tour the facilities just a few days later. After his tour, he stated the Negro ward might be immediately useful since it was the newest, being built in 1929 with updates and additions in 1942. Combs suggested a facility for senior citizens since Jefferson County had the largest number of aged people in the state. His main reason was the proximity to Central State Hospital at Lakeland. He felt the main building could house up to 800 senior citizens, well above the number suggested earlier. A Special House committee was formed and reported the property could be usable in a short time. The committee recommended the state purchase the property since it was structurally sound, in good repair and had ample grounds. County Judge Marlow Cook also supported the proposal. If the property could be sold or leased to the state, a non-profit agent, patients living there could receive federal and state assistance. On April 11, 1962, the state agreed to take over the proposed center to serve the indigent seniors in the state.

> **Waverly Hills was used by the Red Cross when a devastating flood hit the Louisville area in the 1960's.**

Waverly Hills Geriatric Center would open in October as a non-profit center for the elderly, leased from the state by the Kentucky Geriatric Foundation. As part of a $312,500 renovation project, the center would paint the rooms, corridors and porches pastel colors. Handrails were added along walls and radiators were covered to guard against falls and burns. The doors were widened for wheelchairs and special showers and tubs were installed. Dr. John C. Wong of Toronto was hired as Director. Wong had a long history of elderly care and his proposals for the center seemed hopeful. Wong felt the center should cater to both the physically fit and chronically ill. He planned to include musical therapy as treatment and to build a mini-golf range, a woodworking shop and cottages for the married seniors. Unfortunately, Wong, a Canadian citizen, had to leave the country before any of his dreams could be realized. Albert

> In 1960, a 42-year old Jeffersontown father was sentenced to a year in jail and a $500 fine by the Juvenile Court after refusing to accept treatment for an advanced case of tuberculosis. Charles T. Hood was given the maximum penalty for the charge of contributing to dependency of his four children. Hood had been admitted to Waverly four times. All four times he left against the medical advice of the staff. Hood had a far advanced and active case of tuberculosis and was constantly exposing his children.

Bordonaro was hired to replace Wong. Bordonaro had little training and experience in only two other hospitals, neither as an administrator.

However, by all accounts, Waverly Geriatric Center, the only one like it in the nation, continued on as before: helping those who need help the most. Daily care for the 200 patients was provided by 26 doctors, a psychiatrist, 7 registered nurses and 15 practical nurses.

Residents, all over the age of 62, had a library, beauty parlor, barber shop, used-clothing office, dentist's office, garden, two cafeterias and large auditorium for dances and movies. In the two arts and crafts shops, residents enjoyed making quilts, lamps, rugs, and tile pictures. All items were sold in the gift shop and the monies helped to pay for activities for the residents.

Waverly charged $100 per month for independent seniors; $150 for those needing personal care; $200 for those needing nursing care.

Plans for the park were under way as well. Landscape architect Hilbert Dahl designs included a 9-hole golf course, 8-acre lake stocked with bluegill and catfish, swimming beach, 12 tennis courts, bridle path and a $130,000 community center and clubhouse. Another 273 acres were sold in 1962 for $182,350. Monies for building the park would cost another $175,000.

Waverly Park was dedicated on June 4, 1966 by County Judge Marlow Cook. 350 citizens showed up for the ceremony. Cook released the "Waverly Whale" into the lake as part of the celebration. This 5-pound catfish was tagged and the lucky winner who caught him would get a trophy to commemorate the event.

In 1968, a federal grant from the US Public Health Service in the amount of $415,467 paved the wave for an outpatient and emergency care center to open on Waverly grounds. The center was called Waverly Mental Health-Mental Retardation Center and employed 58 full-time and 26 part-time employees including psychiatrists, psychologists, social workers, nurses, therapists, clerical personnel and aides. The center served the counties of Jefferson, Henry, Bullitt, Trimble, Oldham, Spencer and Shelby.

In 1970, Waverly Hills Geriatric Center was renamed Woodhaven Medical Services. The name reflected the more comprehensive facility and removed the stigma of the public institution. The institution was a privately-owned governing body, the Kentucky Geriatric Foundation, who leased the building from the state for $1 a year. The institution changed regulations to begin accepting patients as young as 18 (the previous age was 62). The facility had 192 nursing beds and 177 personal care beds.

In August, 1980, The Courier-Journal reported that a resident confined to a wheelchair died after falling off a loading dock. The 85-year old Claude Lefter, partially blind had come down an elevator, pushed his wheelchair through a hallway to a loading dock. His chair tumbled over edge to a parking lot 5 feet below. Lefter died of head injuries. State investigators ruled the death an 'unforeseeable accident'. Woodhaven officials immediately installed a door to block the corridor leading to loading dock.

However, the incident caught the attention of Sharon Ware, State Director of Licensing and Regulation and she made a surprise visit to Woodhaven in August.

Ware's report, called a statement of deficiencies, found 47 violations, including the following incidents: puddles of urine in the halls and rooms; dried feces on chairs, sheets and floors; roaches crawling on patients and wheelchairs; patients locked and bolted in their rooms; sparse accommodations were available in the rooms including only a bed, bedside table and chair; dirty linen; rooms were too small to meet government regulations; lack of air-conditioning or carpeting in any of the rooms; the rooms were too far from the nursing stations; many rooms had no bathrooms; lack of documentation for medication; cold food served to patients; improperly labeled and stored liquid foods; overcrowding in patients' rooms; dirty urinals sitting next to water pitchers; dirty bedside commodes; improper care of patients with dirty feet and ankles; patients with dirty and long fingernails; exposed patients; inadequate medical records; underweight and thirsty patients; poorly kept and falsified records; and unattended patients, some left alone untended for hours.

Further investigations showed that Woodhaven had lost more than $82,000 in 1979 and it was discovered that the center was in the top 10 for the home with the most complaint investigations, with over ten reports made. Findings showed that six of those were at least partially justified, including understaffing and poor housekeeping.

Based on Ware's report, Woodhaven received a highly critical list of patient care violations and state agencies decided not to place any more wards of the state at the home. Ware recommended the immediate closure of the facility, the first time a skilled-care home had ever been recommended for closure.

David Wilson, administrator, refuted the claims and said many patients, less than 20%, were locked up on doctor's orders so they wouldn't wander away. Wilson insisted the center would need 45 more people if patients were allowed to wander freely. Wilson also stated that many patients were kept only behind

Dutch doors, which divided in half with the top left open.

Woodhaven was ordered to submit a plan for correcting the violations within 10 days. Geriatrics Foundations head, Thomas L. Ray, insisted the state was simply hassling Woodhaven and that the renovations called for would cost up to $600,000-money that was not available. Ray insisted he would have to tear down the building and construct a brand new facility to be in compliance. Ray questioned why the waiver, given to older buildings if they provide good care and didn't endanger the patients, couldn't continue. After all, the waivers had been in effect for 18 years. Ray insisted he would need 2-3 years to correct the list of violations.

In September, the state began making plans to close Woodhaven. On September 17, the State Certificate of Need and Licensure Board voted unanimously to close one of the state's largest elderly centers. The Board refused to waive the licensing requirements. All 200 patients, mostly on Medicaid, would be forced to relocate.

Ray responded in the newspaper, "It'll be a cold day in hell before we lay down and die."

On September 20, a spokesman for the Department of Human Resources stated that Woodhaven had submitted a plan for improvement. The Department approved the plan and a momentary stay was issued. That same day, employees and patients, many in wheelchairs, picketed outside Woodhaven carrying signs that read "State Stinks".

On October 1, under the provisions of the Adult Protective Services Act and without notice, state officials transferred 25 patients to facilities around Kentucky. All 25 were wards of the state. Approximately 7 patients weighed less than 70 pounds. Some were not dressed; some were tied to their chairs with sheets. Two were hospitalized at University Hospital, too sick to be moved.

As the private ambulances pulled up to take the patients away, Wilson told reporters he would not release them until a court order plus a valid legal statement was presented. A state attorney quickly obtained statements. Wilson acceded, stating he wanted to avoid legal issues.

Wilson also said that 'transfer trauma' was likely to occur for many of the patients-a psychological condition that can affect patients when suddenly moved to unfamiliar surroundings. Wilson warned the shock could prove fatal. He said the state should have prepared the patients over several days, interviewing them and describing new surroundings. Ware disagreed, citing questioning whether the recent picket and protest didn't also fall under the same category. Ware said she had notified Woodhaven's doctor. Ware insisted she wanted to avoid a media circus and thought Wilson wouldn't cooperate.

Wilson submitted a $445,000 renovation plan but added that the state was demanding renovations totaling more than $2.5 million. The Kentucky Department of Finance refused the plan.

On December 8, Woodhaven announced it would be closing. Ware pledged to help find housing for the 150 residents. More than 160 employees, some who had been there in the days of the tuberculosis sanatorium, were now suddenly without jobs.

Under the most intense state investigation ever, 150 elderly patients were transferred to other homes and hospitals in the state. While none died from shock, two died from long-term health issues in the next month. 19 showed significant malnourishment and 53 weighed less than 100 pounds. The last ten patients, moving at a rate of 10 per day, left Woodhaven January 1, 1962,

Waverly Hills would lie abandoned for the next twenty years.

In 1983, the property was auctioned and the grounds then purchased from the state by J. Clifford Todd, a Simpsonville-developer who,

> In a short time, graffiti covered nearly every wall in the building. Broken windows and doors made it a dangerous place to explore.

along with Frankfort architect Milton Thompson, planned to operate a prison at the site. When state officials rejected that idea due to public protest, the idea of an apartment complex surfaced. That plan also fell through and the land was divided up into three tracts and sold.

Charles Severs, a physician previously employed at Woodhaven, purchased one of the largest parcels of land-29 acres including the hospital and other buildings-for $128,000 in December of 1986. He hired a consultant about the feasibility of turning the hospital into a retirement community with renovations estimated to cost between $6-10 million. The 190-apartment retirement community was to have been called 'Grandview Resort' and would offer residents a library, cafeteria, and tennis courts. However, the idea was later rejected by the consultant because of the high cost of renovation and lack of an elderly population in southwest Jefferson County who could not afford the proposed monthly rent of $400-700.

The other two parcels were sold to Mack Dickerson of Glasgow, KY and Milton Thompson. Thompson bought the southernmost tract bordering East Pages Lane and the Bobby Nichols Golf Course for $152,000. Dickerson, a lumberman, bought a forty acre parcel to the north for $70,000.

It was during Severs' ownership that Waverly Hills slipped into decay. Security guards reported robbers taking truckloads of copper plumbing supplies, breaking windows and doors, and littering the area with tires. Severs had trouble keeping the property in good condition stating it cost approximately $20,000 per year just to maintain

the property with a caretaker, taxes, utilities, maintenance, and insurance.

In March 1996, Robert Alberhasky, a Louisville internist, bought the Waverly Hills property from Severs. Alberhasky was part of Christ The Redeemer Foundation, Inc. and had plans to build the world's tallest statue of Jesus on the hill overlooking Dixie highway. In addition to the statue, an arts and worship center and a meditation garden was also planned. This project was to have been based on the famous Christ the Redeemer statue on Corcovado Mountain in Rio De Janeiro, Brazil. This statue stands 125 feet tall and is located on top of the 2300-foot mountain overlooking the city. The sculpture was to have been completed by locally-renowned artist Ed Hamilton and designed by

architect Jasper Ward. The landscape design was submitted by the architect firm of Frederick Law Olmstead from New York.

According to an article in *The Courier-Journal* (March 1996), the first phase of the project was to have cost $4 million. Once completed the statue would have stood 150-feet tall and 150-feet wide, mounted on the roof of the sanatorium. At a total height of 270 feet above the ground, the statue would have been the tallest religious figure in the world. A second phase would have taken Waverly and converted it into a chapel, theatre and gift shop-called the "Life Center Complex". This phase would have cost another $8 million.

Alberhasky organized Waverly Hope, a foundation who wanted a give the community "a universal center for  inspirational activity". Fundraising efforts began and Alberhasky spoke at local churches and published ads in the newspapers.

According to the 'Waverly Hope Foundation' brochure, the theme for the movement was called "Welcome the World with Open Arms". The project was to have been a serene and meditative center with access for all denominations. Alberhasky's objective was to "give the community a universal center for inspirational activity". The plans included a chapel, theater, and museum with exhibits of Christian history. Alberhasky also hoped the center would be a focus for social outreach, education and artistic programs. Alberhasky's plan was for Louisville to become a "City of Hope".

While initial enthusiasm was promising, many did not buy into Alberhasky's vision and his plans did not materialize. After a year, only $3000 was raised towards the effort according to The Kentucky Post (December 12, 1997). The plan was eventually canceled in December of 1997 and Alberhasky was forced to abandon the project.

Alberhasky abandoned the project and wanted to have the building condemned. Apparently, his plan was to redevelop the site and possibly raze the buildings, allowing a cellular phone tower to replace the existing structures. His notion was denied by the county because Waverly was a historic building, being listed on the National Register August 12, 1983.

It is during this time period that Waverly began to decline to its present state of disrepair.

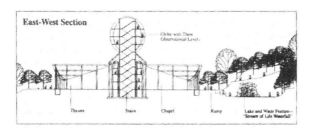

> **An interview with Ed Hamilton, Louisville sculptor and author**
>
> "Bob would talk to us about his visit to the statue in Brazil. He said we needed something here [in Louisville] to give us inspiration. It would have been fascinating to put this huge statue on the highest hill in Louisville and you could have seen it for miles. People would have come from all around the country to partake of its healing powers. When I showed my doodles to Bob, he loved it. He said it was free and uninhibited and exactly what he wanted. When I looked at the property, I could only think about how much work it was going to take to get the property ready. But Bob was enthusiastic; he had more enthusiasm than anyone I'd ever seen. It was going to be beautiful, in the woods on top of that hill. I was going to make it out of stainless steel. When the light hit it, it would have sparkled for miles and miles. People were excited in the beginning, but somewhere along the way it just died."

In 2002, the building was included in a list of the "Most Endangered Properties" by the Louisville Historical League and Preservation Society.

## Chapter Nine
## A Place to Call Home:
## The Buildings of Waverly Hills

These tennis courts at Waverly were not used by the patients; tennis would have been much too strenuous. Instead, doctors and employees used this amenity. The courts are no longer in operation.

Many people think of Waverly as simply the one gothic hospital building but, in reality, the campus was huge and spread out over several hundred acres. Although the original plot of land was fairly small, Waverly would add acreage over the years as their need for more buildings and land would increase. One noted land purchase occurred in 1929 when 160 acres was added. The property was a farm owned by the Hoertz family and located near Arnoldtown Pike. This property was used primarily as a dairy for the hospital. In 1933, 500 acres would be purchased by the hospital and an 18 car garage was built. The building and land purchase was a PWA (Public Works Administration) project.

In addition to the hospital, Waverly Hills also offered at least three clinics in the Louisville area so that nurses could more easily test for the disease. At the downtown Louisville clinic, free fluoroscopes, a type of X-ray, were offered to area children.

## 1. Employee's Quarters

Many different types of employees were needed at Waverly including nurses, doctors, farmers, orderlies, housekeeping staff and countless others. Since the location, at that time, was so distant, a housing unit was needed. This farmhouse located on the property was originally reserved for the Medical Director but was soon converted into housing for the ever-growing staff. The employees' quarters were located at the original entrance to Waverly Hills. This building is no longer in existence.

## 2. Laundry Room

This is one of few buildings that has survived the test of time. These rooms are connected to the main hospital through underground tunnels that run underneath the road between the two buildings. The tunnel aisles are wide so that the massive amounts of laundry could be carted between the buildings. Late in the 19th century it was standard practice to burn nearly everything the patient owned or touched. However, once the public became more knowledgeable about germs and how they were spread, this practice was abandoned. The laundry house was an addition to the main hospital, constructed in 1930 at a cost of $10,000. The laundry room is currently used as a gift shop and lobby area as well as an audio-visual center that shows an introductory movie for those who tour the building.

## 3. Negro Division of Waverly Hills Sanatorium

Waverly was not alone in offering a separate treatment center for African Americans. Most large hospitals in other states had similar practices

and had different buildings for blacks and many hospitals had separate "Colored Wards". Waverly was well ahead of other states who often resorted to barbaric means of treating blacks as those states also used mental hospitals and even penitentiaries to treat African Americans. In one of the worst instances, Maryland Hospital in Spring Grove used canvas tents to treat black patients in both summer and winter, although TB victims would be brought to the main hospital during heavy storms or freezing weather. Some hospitals refused to treat African Americans outright and it was left to family members to provide for care and comfort.

Consumption was a cause of death in at least one in five African Americans, an average four to five times greater than the white population of the time. In the 1940's, over 25% of the patients admitted to Waverly would be black although 42% of the deaths were from this same group. Many wealthy white victims would contract the disease from black servants and it is largely because of this that focus began to shift to this under-served segment of the population.

> **Negro Health Week** was held annually in April in the 1920's and 30's. In 1931, the death rate for blacks in Louisville was 258 deaths per 100,000 compared to just 75 for whites. Leaflets were distributed through the 'colored' branches of the public libraries, at the YWCA and at local movie theatres. The pamphlets would emphasize healthy eating and hygiene habits.

An addition to the building was added in 1932 at a cost of $35,000.

Eventually the death rate for whites in the area would decline but black TB victims would continue to be the hardest hit segment of the population. A new employee building was to have been slated for construction in 1942 but a report from that same year showed that there was a lack of adequate provision for black patients. A doctor at the time, urging for upgrades, insisted renovations were essential because of the "Negros' greater susceptibility to disease, general lack of ability to pay for treatment and closeness of the relationships with the white population. The same report also showed that the average length of stay for white patients was 414 days compared to just 259 for the black patients. Since many were being dismissed too soon, they were only infecting the population and generally had to return for more treatment. The death rate during this same time was 17% for white patients and 48% for black.

Once the public found out about the dire situation through media coverage, pressure was put on officials and the building project was instead created for black tuberculosis victims. This would increase the beds by another 96. Even so, there was often a waiting list for blacks in the overcrowded unit while there were many available vacant beds in the white division.

The black patients would be treated by African-American doctors and nurses, some of the first in the United States to be trained to deal with the disease. The Negro Ward had its own gift shop as well, run by Louis Matthew, a blind tuberculosis patient with only one leg. Matthews would run the store for many years.

The Negro Ward burned to the ground on November 22, 1970. More than 75 volunteers from four Jefferson County fire departments worked to contain the fire but the blaze gutted the building. The building had been abandoned since 1962 and while arson was suspected, it was never proven. David Wilson, administrator of the property, stated to local newspapers that he had run off teenagers that same day. This building no longer exists and condominiums have been built over the site although some original foundation stones remain.

### 4. Children's Pavilion

The children's pavilion did not offer treatment services for all ages of children. The main hospital reserved its fifth floor to treat those youngest victims, children too small to be placed in a ward

> Many young children ended up at Waverly as orphans when their mothers would die shortly after their births. Waverly was the only place they knew as home, the only mothers they knew the nurses who tended them.

situation. The children's pavilion also served as a sort of orphanage for those unfortunate enough to have parents who were stricken with tuberculosis.

Once a child had been exposed to the disease and a parent admitted to Waverly, the child was brought in for examination and observation. If the child showed signs of the disease, it could be caught early and treated. Tuberculosis in children was the easiest to treat. Healthy orphans would either be sent to live with other family members or, if none existed, then care was provided through the Kentucky Children's Home or the Protestant Orphan's Home on Bardstown Road.

While rest and recuperation were top priority, children at Waverly still had to attend school and, for fun, could play on the playground as seen in the picture above. Outdoor swings, see-saws, trapezes, and slides kept the youth busy. Waverly Hill Sanatorium School also accepted a small number of children from the county. Jefferson County and the City of Louisville Boards of Education split the expenses for the teacher's salary. The Parent Teacher Association of Jefferson County furnished books and other needed supplies.

In the 1930's over 81 children were patients at Waverly Hills. Twelve of those were below school age and six were babies aged six months to four

> **The Council of Jewish Women often hosted yearly birthday parties at Waverly where gifts of much needed clothes and shoes were given. Women's clubs around Louisville regularly sent clothes to the children year-round.**

years. The remainder would be expected to spend four and a half hours per day in school with as much time as possible spent outdoors. Classes at the school ranged from first through the eighth grades. The rest of the day would be spent resting.

Bedtime for the children was 8 pm and each child would be awakened at 6 am. Daily rest breaks in bed were required, as they were for adults, from 1 to 3 pm and from 5 to 6 pm. When children were not resting, playing or learning, they were expected to help with some household duties including making their bed, looking after their own lavatories and helping with some of the smaller children. Weekly chores included delivering the Waverly newspaper to buildings and rooms around the campus.

The original Children's Pavilion was built in 1915 and housed 40 children. A 150-bed unit was built in 1930 at a cost of $153,000. The pavilion was closed in 1942. These buildings are no longer in existence.

> **The average life span for a male was 45 years of age in 1875.**

### 5. Men's Ward

In the early days, men and women at Waverly were not encouraged to fraternize unnecessarily and were kept separated on hospital grounds. The theory of the time was that socializing among the sexes would cause increased blood pressure and excitement and most tuberculosis victims were not allowed to engage in any activity that might overexcite them. But, many stories exist of young girls sneaking out of the hospital in order to meet their beaus, as well as countless stories of men and women who met at Waverly and then went on to marry.

Most of the patients at Waverly were women although it was not a women's only hospital. The overrepresentation of females might have more to do with prevailing social theory at the time. Remember that tuberculosis was seen as a delicate disease reserved for the romantic and tender of soul. Also, many men would refuse to admit they had the disease, fearful of abandoning their family, most of who depended solely on the husband for monetary existence. Left with few choices, many simply were reluctant to get care. While men certainly suffered from the disease as often as women, by the time the disease was acknowledged, it might have been too late.

Many of the men brought in for treatment were factory workers, the hardest career hit. Little, if any, regulations existed at the time and men working in local factories would breathe in dust and polluted air daily, lowering their resistance and speeding up the effects of the disease. Many efforts would be directed towards the industrial workers at such area businesses as Louisville Textile Mills, one of the largest factories in the area. Physicians and nurses from Waverly would often visit giving instructive talks.

> In 1941, the average cost per day of caring for a TB patient at Waverly Hills was $2.10.

As the disease progressed and social climate changed, men and women were admitted in the general hospital. This building is no longer in existence although some of the original foundation still exists.

### 6. Nurse's Dormitory

Because tuberculosis was such a contagious disease, the nursing staff was asked to stay on the grounds of the hospital so as not to spread tuberculosis in the general public. Since a typical work week for the nurses was 6 and ½ days per week, there would have been little time for return visits home anyway. The original nurses' home was in the old Hays' farmhouse, the house of the original owner of the property.

As more and more patients were admitted, more nurses were needed and many would share the TB hospital with the patients. As the epidemic raged, more staff would be needed and Waverly would build a state-of-the-art facility to house the nurses in 1928 at a cost of $75,000. The architect of the building was JC Murphy of DX Murphy and

Brother. In addition to their rooms, the nurses' dormitory had its own kitchen and laundry facility.

Nurses did become infected with tuberculosis while working and statistics of the time state that there was a 1 in 4 chance of becoming infected for anyone living or working closely with a TB victim. While some of the nurses became infected while caring for their patients, these courageous women did not let that fact stop them. Nurses of that time left behind their families and friends for a virtual quarantine on top of the hill at Waverly. Many would become infected and die; some would meet future husbands and go on to lead productive, healthy lives; still more would spend their entire careers working at Waverly, and later at Woodhaven Geriatric Center. The original building no longer exists.

> **In 1940, Waverly Hills offered Kentucky military authorities the use of all its X-ray machines to be used for the recruits who were being called up for active duty for World War II.**

### 7. Fresh Water Pump House

This small building was responsible for supplying fresh water to the hospital and was only used until city water became available. Pure limestone water was pumped from driven wells located on the property.

The need for city water became greater as more and more patients were received at Waverly Hills. The pumped water was too hard for the steam heating and the pipes rapidly filled with a thick limestone coating that would have to be periodically removed. In addition, the water was too hard for the daily laundry purposes and had to be chemically treated before the linens could be washed. The city water extension to Waverly Sanatorium was completed in December of 1928 at a cost of $116,000. This building is no longer in existence.

## 8. Sewage Treatment

Waverly's sewage disposal, an Imhoff sewage disposal plant, was quite advanced for the time period. This small building was responsible for treating the sewage at Waverly and was only used until service was provided by the county. This building is no longer in existence.

## 9. Boiler Room and Steam Tunnel

Technically, the steam tunnel wasn't a separate building but is one of the few structures left that still exists at Waverly. The tunnel was originally built to supply steam from the boiler rooms and power plant located at the bottom of the hill to the hospital. For the first Waverly hospital, the original wooden structure, individual power plants were built next to the buildings and coal would have to be brought up the hill. As Waverly was being enhanced in the 1920's, a more efficient system was the railtrack system. A switch was added from the Illinois Central Railroad to

> In 1930, 450 patients were housed at Waverly. 80 of those were children and 85 of those, African American.

the powerhouse. Over 75 carloads of coal would be used annually to supply the hospital with power.

The workers also discovered it was an efficient and quicker way to access the hospital and began to use it to haul supplies up and down. In its early days, the steam tunnel was used by the employees who wanted to keep warm on the long walk from the parking area at the bottom of the hill.

The original steam tunnel was approximately 400 feet long with only one entrance and exit, both locked securely although the tunnel was kept open for years and local children growing up in the area

> In the 1950's the Women's Advisory Board at Waverly Hills gave a fully furnished five room brick house to the hospital. The house had two bedrooms, a screened porch and terrace and was used by the family of Dr. Fernando Desneres, a doctor at Waverly. Other gifts from the Advisory Board, totaling over $24,000, were an elevator in the Negro Ward and an electric cable for x-rays. The Board has also refurnished and redecorated all the hospital waiting rooms and solariums, the medical director's office and all staff rooms as well as supplying clothing for children and adults, donating typewriters for the educational unit and providing two movies for patients each month. The Board also maintained the "Waverly Shop", the local gift shop, and furnished it with gifts, refreshments, needles, and other needed items. The Board had always been a major presence at the hospital and some members remember running a sandwich hut for construction workers when the hospital was still being built.

remember using it to warm up on chilly winter days.

The tunnel had one side with steps leading down and the other side with a smooth stone slab, as seen in the picture. The stone slab originally had tracks running along its length and moved supplies up and down the tunnel, similar to coal cars.

The tunnel is one of the most famous and most asked about features at Waverly and has become known locally as the "Death Tunnel" or "Body Chute". At the peak of the TB epidemic, the tunnel was used for another purpose. When multiple deaths began occurring at Waverly, the nursing staff felt that the site of hearses parked out front was not good for patients who were trying to recover. Eventually the staff decided to use the old steam tunnel to transport dead bodies to the bottom of the hill where the hearses could pick them up, unseen by the eyes of the hopeful patients. Rather than use the coal carts, the table gurneys at the hospital had wheels and the deceased would be lowered to the bottom of the hill using a system of pulleys and winches. The power house addition was added to the main hospital in 1930 at a cost of $50,000.

| Daily Cost for TB treatment at Waverly | |
|---|---|
| 1911 | $1.16 |
| 1912 | $1.12 |
| 1913 | $1.54 |
| 1914 | $1.48 |
| 1915 | $1.30 |

No pictures exist of two other known buildings-the entertainment pavilion attached to the original hospital and the barn used for the farm animals. Most of the original buildings have been demolished and only 3 are still in use: Waverly Hospital, the Steam Tunnel and the Laundry Room.

## Chapter Ten
## The Pioneers:
## Important Louisvillians in the Fight Against Tuberculosis

<u>Esther Maxwell Barrens</u> was an African-American and served as the Head Nurse Supervisor of the Negro Division of Waverly Hills Sanatorium. Barrens began working as the supervisor of nurses in 1926. She was one of the first graduates of Meharry School of Nursing in 1906 and later served as a Member of the Executive Board of the Meharry Alumni Association of the school's Parent-Teacher Association. There was often a shortage of nurses in the hospital and she would often be the only nurse on duty. This pushed Barnes to begin training nurses. Barrens also advocated for black children in the hospital to receive education and to be included in the activities of the other children. Barrens would work for Waverly Hills for over 28 years. Barrens died August 14, 1954.

> Willie Miller was the Grounds Superintendent at Waverly Hills for over 35 years beginning in the 1930's.

> Mrs. Margaret B. Pusey was the Superintendent of Nurses for 31 years ending with her retirement in 1945.

**Dr. Jesse Burnett Bell** was born in Louisiana in 1904. After graduating from Morehouse College in Atlanta and Meharry Medical Center in Nashville, he moved to Frankfort, Kentucky and opened a private practice. In 1935, Dr. Bell would move to Louisville and become the first African American doctor to practice medicine at Waverly Hills. During his lifetime, Dr. Bell was on the Board of Trustees at Mount Lebanon Baptist Church; served as the Vice Chairman of the Louisville Urban League; was a member of Jefferson County Medical Society, Falls City Medical Association, the American Heart Association, the Bureau of Health

This picture was found in the first Board of Tuberculosis Report, circa 1910. The baby is purported to be the first baby ever born at Waverly. According to the report, the mother was admitted with more than 33 open lesions in her lungs. Her baby was born six weeks premature. Both mother and child survived and were regaining their health at the time the photo was taken.

Service for Kentucky; and served on the Kentucky Commission on Higher Education. In October of 1965, Jesse Bell became the first African American to serve on the University of Louisville Board of Overseers. He is buried in Cave Hills Cemetery in Louisville, Kentucky.

> **Medical Directors of Waverly Hills**
> Dr. A.M. Forster 1910
> Dr. Dunning S. Wilson 1910-1917
> Dr. John B. Floyd 1917-1918
> Dr. E.L. Pirkey (Acting Director) 1918
> Dr. Oscar O. Miller 1918-1930
> Dr. B.L. Brock 1930-1945
> Dr. Alvin B. Mullen 1945-1961

**Abram Hite (A.H.) Bowman** was born in Kentucky and moved to Louisville in 1903 after seeking adventure in Alaska. He set up a hay and grain business that would later convert to a freight transfer company. For twenty years, he was president of that company, the A.H. Bowman Transfer Company, a large organization of the time that employed over 130 men. He was also president of Bowman Wrecking Company. In his youth, he suffered frequent respiratory and pleurisy infections which he later learned was brought on by tuberculosis. Bowman would travel to the renowned Saranac Lake, NY tuberculosis clinic and receive successful treatment. It is through his experiences with tuberculosis that led him to be such an advocate for the consumptive sufferers in his home county. The service he provided for the hospital as Board member was non-remunerative. He was greatly interested in aeronautics and that interest would lead to his partnership in the Bowman-Park Aero, Co. He established an airfield on Taylorsville Road that would eventually become known as Bowman Field and would maintain the field during much of his lifetime at his own expense. He would be called by many the "Father of Louisville Aviation". He was also a member of Shriners, Board of Trade, the Transportation Club, and Louisville Boat Club as well as serving as President of Morris Plan Bank. In 1925, he was selected as "Louisville's Most Useful Citizen" by the Kiwanis Club, mostly due to his tireless work at Waverly Hills. He died at 68 of a heart attack on July 20, 1943. He is buried in Cave Hill Cemetery in Louisville, Kentucky.

> Alvin B. Mullen, the last Medical Director at Waverly, would work for the hospital over 29 years, beginning as a doctor. His employment was briefly interrupted as he served time in the military. Upon his release, he returned to Waverly.

**Oscar O. Miller**, originally from New South Wales, Australia and a1911 graduate of the University of Louisville, became famous at the hospital for asking patients if they were happy. During his lifetime, he was Kentucky Medical Association President, received a distinguished service award, was president of the Kentucky and Jefferson County medical societies, president of Executives Club, president of Lion's Club, member of the Board of Trustees for University of Louisville, charter member of Board for Louisville

Tuberculosis Association, and medical director of Waverly Hills and Hazelwood. He would also teach at the University of Louisville Medical School and teach Sunday school at First Christian Church. He had five sons, two of whom became doctors. Dr. Miller is the fourth from the left in this staff photo taken in front of Waverly Hills.

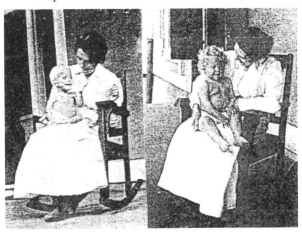

This before and after picture showcases the dramatic way the simple treatments at Waverly was indeed a matter of life and death for many. The baby seen here, named Virginia, weighed only 12 lbs. when she was admitted to Waverly. She was expected to die. After a course of treatments, Virginia's weight increased to over 30 lbs. Her nickname was "Pet of the San".

**Dr. Maurine Pelham Redden** became the first, and only, African American tuberculosis specialist female doctor in the nation when she was named Negro Division Resident Physician at Waverly Hills. At the time of her appointment, Dr. Redden was a member of the School of Medicine faculty at Howard University. She was married to Captain James Redden of the Army Air Force. Redden received her BS degree in 1938 and MD in 1939 from Howard. From 1939-1940, she interned and was Assistant Resident in Internal Medicine at Freeman's Hospital in Washington, DC where she was originally from. From 1941-1943, she was Chief Resident Physician on the tuberculosis staff at Freeman's. In 1944, she was studying at Herman Kiefer Hospital, Detroit, on a Rockefeller Fellowship at the time of her appointment to Waverly Hills.

> Mary Hodges became the first Nurse from Waverly Hills to join the Navy. In 1942, Hodges joined the reserves and was assigned to the Great Lakes Naval Training Station in Michigan.

**S.A. Rusker**, the last administrator of Waverly Hills, would die within on the grounds of Waverly Hills. Prior to Waverly, Rusker was consultant to Kentucky State Tuberculosis Hospital Commission and to the Battle Creek, Michigan Health Center and Madison, Tennessee Hospital and Sanatorium. He was elected first Vice-President of 4500-member American College of Hospital Administrators and was a Speaker for American Youth Lecture Bureau. In 1960, he was named "Hospital Administrator of the Year" by the Kentucky Hospital Association. Rusker served as chairman of Institutional Council for Louisville

Fire Prevention Bureau, Trustee of Kentucky Physicians Mutual (Blue Shields) and Chairman of Fiscal Court's Medical Center Steam Plant Operating Committee. Rusker was the founder and president of the Western Kentucky Hospital Council, president of Kentucky State Hospital Administration, administrator of Paducah City Hospital and a member of American Hospital Association. A native of Barnesville, Minnesota, he was married with 3 kids. Rusker died Wednesday, November 2$^{nd}$, 1961 and was buried in Louisville Memorial Gardens.

---

**William M. Jordan**
**Chief Engineer at Waverly Hills**

---

In 1943, William V. Jordan built the first portable lung-photographing machine in Louisville. The X-ray machine differed from regular version in that it used 35-mm film and could take over 100 x-rays an hour. The film was also much cheaper and the machine could be assembled in 10 minutes, allowing examinations all over the city. The first to be X-rayed on the machine were Kentucky hotel employees and food handlers. Jordan worked on the machine for 3 years. William Jordan was also responsible for Waverly Hills being the first hospital in the world to have radio headphones hooked up to hospital bed. The headphones were installed on every bed in 1921 in the main hospital and patients listened to Jordan's radio station, WLAP, as well as church sermons and even educational services.

Cave Hill Cemetery in Louisville, established in 1846, is the burying ground for many notable Waverly Hills pioneers including A.H. Bowman, Thomas H. Hays, Dr. Jesse Burnett Bell, E.L Pirkey and countless other tuberculosis victims and Waverly Hills staff. Dr. John C. Croghan, of the Mammoth Cave tuberculosis experiment, was originally interred at his ancestral home Locust Grove but the remains of the Croghan family were moved to Cave Hill in 1916.

Some tuberculosis victims were buried on Waverly Hills's property. Their bodies now lie in unmarked graves, kept highly secret, so that they may rest in peace.

## Chapter Eleven:
## A Bright Future
## Waverly Hills Today

You can find a lot of interesting things on Ebay. But a haunted house? That's exactly how Charlie Mattingly came to learn that Waverly Hills Sanatorium was up for sale. Charlie and his wife Tina grew up with the legend on the hill. Mattingly's father would often tell him when he was a small boy, "You just don't want to go up there, whatever you do. It's a bad place." Of course that did little to dissuade Charlie Mattingly. If anything, it made his curiosity grow.

Many original fixtures can still be seen in Waverly such as these tables in the morgue.

When Mattingly mentioned the abandoned property to his father, a story started to unravel that showed Mattingly how close his connection to the abandoned building really was. "I grew up hearing stories about this place my whole life and I never came up here. When I heard it was for sale, I mentioned it to my father. He started telling me all these stories about *his* time here." That was a surprise to Mattingly who never knew his father had once both worked and been a patient at Waverly Hills Tuberculosis

Sanatorium. Mattingly's father had actually worked at Waverly Hills when he was a young man in the 1930's in the cafeteria.

> Each October Waverly is home to a huge haunted house, the largest in Louisville.

He earned $1 a day, but only got to keep 25 cents. The other 75 was sent home to help care for a family that included six brothers on a farm in Meade County.

"At that time, it was a tremendous opportunity because he wasn't eighteen yet. He stayed for almost two years and started to get the symptoms of TB. He saw all the doctors and nurses living here who had caught tuberculosis. He got scared, especially when they started asking him to take meals into the patients' rooms. The details are a little sketchy on this next part, but he somehow developed a hole in his chest because of a treatment at the hospital. He was scared to stay, so he ran away. He was afraid that if he stayed, they would stick him with the other TB patients and he would die. He went back to Meade County and lived through it."

When Mattingly and his father made their first visit to the old hospital, it was in shambles. There were no doors or windows. "I looked over at my dad and I could tell he was getting really upset. My dad was not an emotional guy. You would never see him cry. When we started walking around, he would point out to me where other buildings used to be. When we came up to the door and started to walk in, he got tears in his eyes. He said, 'I can't walk in. I can't take it. I would rather remember it the way it was.' We just left."

Mattingly thought that was probably the end of the deal but the real estate agent called him back and encouraged him to make an offer because the seller was very motivated to get rid of the property. "The way I picture it now is like when you're watching those old cartoons when the safe falls on someone's head. That's how I got this place."

The more Mattingly learned about the building, the more attached to it he became. "Waverly Hills was  built as a sanatorium, not a sanitarium. It was a place where people went to get well.

"After we purchased it we found out that we walked into a hornet's nest with all the city departments that had problems with the building- no doors, no windows. After I fixed a few things, I found out nobody was allowed in the building because of the binding elements. It was hazardous because of the asbestos. The public wasn't supposed to be in the building at all. Then we had trespassers all over the place. It took us two years of mostly just keeping vagrants out of the building." Removing the asbestos was just one the many renovations that had to be done.

However, all the added security measures would not be enough to deter ghost hunters. "We found out in October the first year that groves of people would come and go through the building because they had been doing it for years. We had to keep them out, though, because if someone got hurt in there, we could have gotten sued. We found out in the very first year that we had it that we couldn't keep the people away from it. We had to keep guards standing all around the building, everywhere, just to keep them out. It was that popular in the local area. *This* is what you do at Halloween time."

It didn't take long for Mattingly to turn that bit of trouble into good news for Waverly Hills. "We just got this great idea-'Hold on!' I found a guy who made some haunted house signs and we made just a small haunted house. We had no idea it would take off the way it did. Everybody and their brothers were coming!" Mattingly gave a percentage of the profits from the haunted house to local charities, an act he continues to this day.

**Renovations on the property continue to this day.**

By opening up Waverly Hills, Mattingly has also improved life in the local community. "We've run out all the vagrants and gangs. Police were always making runs up here-gangs fighting each other, somebody hurt or having to go to the hospital, somebody killed or murdered. If something rough was going to happen in Valley Station, this was the place for it. I've boarded it up and put doors on it and now we open it up to people who actually want to come through and see it and they're not in danger."

Mattingly knew almost right away that Waverly Hills had some extra features. "I was never a person who believed in paranormal activity. I came up here four years ago and videotaped the place. The camera would act funny and the video went dead. It looked like orbs and lightning bolts and figures going through. When I went home and tried the camera out, it would work fine. When we went to board it up, we started hearing things and we couldn't tell what was making the noise. I couldn't figure out what was going on."

One of Mattingly's first visitors was interested in 'the goings-on'. "We'd only had the place about a month when Fox Family Network called us up. They were out in Hollywood and they had heard about this place. I sent them a video I had taken and they called back and wanted to know if I had altered the film! Like I could! When they came out here, they were mostly looking to do something for entertainment. When they were in here filming, the cameramen got absolutely freaked out. One of the guys dropped his camera, got all upset and left. They had all kinds of problems that night-the film messed up, the batteries went dead."

Mattingly knew exactly what he was doing when he let the camera crews in the doors. "I knew the only way I could ever restore this building was to make it famous."

The interior of the laundry, now the tourist center, before renovations.

Mattingly's plan has worked out great. Waverly Hills Sanatorium is listed as one of the top ten most haunted places on EARTH! That's quite an accomplishment and one that Mattingly is using to his advantage. "When people compliment me on how great the building is looking, I say 'I'm really not doing a great job. The building is doing a great job. It's rebuilding itself.' Every penny that goes into this building, the building made for itself. When the money comes in for the tours, I figure out the best and cheapest way to buy building materials or hire a contractor. That's one reason it's going so slow. We have a lot of volunteers and people just work here between jobs. If you come back here one year from today, you're going to see a lot of progress. We know it's going to cost millions and millions to save this place."

Mattingly did most of the work himself, after his full-time third shift job with a little help from his friends and dedicated volunteers, some who have been with him since Mattingly first began the awesome project. "I say to the groups that come up here, 'Thanks and when you come up here next year, you'll see new windows and you can say, 'I paid for one of those windows.'" Everybody can say, 'I'm a little guy who gets to be part of something big.'

His final plan for the old building is grandiose and one that he thinks the patients from long ago would be proud to see. Mattingly is currently operating the site on a non-profit basis, as part of the Waverly Hills Historical Society. "We're finishing the task of stopping the deterioration. From there, we're going to take every bit of money we can get together and create a development plan. What it amounts to is having meetings to decide what we're going to do and then hiring an architect to draw every square foot of the building. We want to know what it's going to take to get it from this state to a final product."

Mattingly's vision for the final product includes a first floor medical research center, a three-story bed and breakfast and then a restaurant on the top floor with a view looking over Valley Station and across the river into Indiana. "I have people who are asking me now to leave deposits for whenever it gets done."

For Mattingly, Waverly Hills is much more than a haunted house. "Waverly Hills gave to this community so much years ago and now it's giving back again, in one form or another. Back in the '20's, this place saved countless lives, countless people gave their lives here to help others. I wonder if you put an ad in the paper right now that said 'We need nurses for a plague that we don't have a cure for and we need you to come up here and leave your family. You can't go back home and chances are you're going to catch it and you're going to die.' How many doctors and nurses do you think would show up? But they did it. We have to pass that story on. Somebody did this. They're gone now but they did this."

## Chapter Twelve
## Grim Prospects:
## Tuberculosis Today

Think tuberculosis has disappeared from the United States? Think again! In 2008, the Centers for Disease Control and Prevention (CDC) reported 12,898 new cases of tuberculosis in the United States. New York has seen one of the biggest increases of tuberculosis infection and health officials have called the situation a full-blown emergency. Many of the cases are among immigrants newly arrived and the homeless, both of whom have difficulty finding and receiving free, quality health care. In 2002, almost 1000 people

---

**A Cure for Tuberculosis?**
Ancient Greeks believed that making a broth from the flesh of a female donkey would cure the sufferer! If that doesn't sound too tasty, how about a brew mixing the ashes of swine dung with raisin wine? How about boa constrictor waste and water?
Cures were little advanced in the early part of the century. Then, it was believed that breathing the breath of an animal would cure the disease.
Drinking the blood of a healthy animal was also considered to have curative effects. Some surmise this is how some folk myths of vampirism got started. There was even one documented police case where a young boy was kidnapped, taken to the home of a wealthy TB sufferer and then cut open so that the innocent blood could be used for a cure.

died in the US from tuberculosis. The District of Columbia has the highest rate of tuberculosis in the nation with North Dakota having the lowest rate.

Currently there are more than 100,000 people in the US with both HIV and TB. For those with AIDS, lowered immunity means greater chance of infection. TB in an AIDS patient is fatal 80% of the time.

A.G. Holley Hospital in Lantana, Florida is the nation's last free-standing tuberculosis hospital that still operates exclusively for tuberculosis treatment.

Tuberculosis still ravages some developing countries such as Africa, Asia and Latin America. Over 90% of new TB cases are occurring in developing nations. The World Health Organization estimates that 70 million people worldwide are infected with TB. Over 8 million people will become ill this year and more than a million of those die

In 1993, WHO reported tuberculosis to be a global emergency.

New strains of tuberculosis are resistant (TB-MDR) to the drugs first discovered in the 1940's. A full course of treatment requires the sufferer to take 10-16 pills every day for up to two years. If an individual does not finish the entire cycle, the TB strain could become resistant. The cost for this cycle can run as high as $2000, an amount equal to the annual income of the countries who suffer the highest infection rate.

Over 70 million deaths from tuberculosis are predicted by 2020. However, the rate of TB infection and spread is declining. Between 1990 and 2010, the rate of new infection dropped nearly 40%.

| WHO (World Health Organization) Fast Facts |
|---|
| - A person with active TB will infect 10-15 people each year.
- TB can lie dormant for years in our bodies before becoming active.
- Somewhere in the world, someone is infected with TB at the rate of one person every second.
- 1/3 of the world's population is infected with TB.
- There were 1.6 million deaths from TB in 2005.
- Africa has the highest mortality rate.
- Some strains of TB are resistant to all known types of anti-TB medication.
- Treating TB with medication can take up to two years.

(Information retrieved from http://www.who.int/en/) |

Photo Credits

Cover photo and inside watermark photo: Mark Ledford (markledford@gmail.com); Photo editing by CC Thomas.

Chapter One: Pg. 10-Ruffer. Studies in the Paleopathology of Egypt (1921). {{PD-old}}; Pg. 12-1871-fashion-class-contrast.gif. Wikipedia; {{PD-old}}; Pg. 13-Janice Carr. Centers for Disease Control (2006) {{PD-USGov }}; Pg. 16-US Department of Health and Human Services (1972) {{PD-USGov-HHS}}.

Chapter Two: Pg. 20-Pluto Springs (1903). {{PD-old}}; Pg. 22-US National Library of Medicine. {{PD-Gov}}; Pg. 27-CC Thomas (2007); Pg. 30-CC Thomas (2007).

Chapter Three: Pg. 32 -CC Thomas (2007); Pg. 34- HUW Williams (2007); Pg. 36-W. Marsh (2000); Pg. 38 -CC Thomas (2007); Pg. 39-CC Thomas (2007); Pg. 42-CC Thomas (2007); Pg. 44-Board of Tuberculosis Hospital Report (1908); Pg. 45-Board of Tuberculosis Hospital Report (1908); Pg. 46-Board of Tuberculosis Hospital Report (1908); Page 48-Board of Tuberculosis Hospital Report (1908).

Chapter Four: Pg. 49-Board of Tuberculosis Hospital Report (1910); Page 52-Board of Tuberculosis Hospital Report (1908); Page 53-Board of Tuberculosis Hospital Report (1910); Pg. 60-University of Louisville Archives (1926); Pg. 62-University of Louisville Archives.

Chapter Five: Pg. 65-University of Louisville Archives; Pg. 66 and 67-University of Louisville Archives; Pg. 79- Louisville Tuberculosis Association (1927); Pg. 80-American Lung Association Christmas Seal (1927).

Chapter Six: Pg. 84-University of Louisville Archives; Pg. 86-University of Louisville Archives; Pg. 88 -Board of Tuberculosis Hospital Report (1908); Pg. 89-Rene Laennec (1825) {{PD-old}}; Pg. 91-University of Louisville Archives; Pg. 93-Board of Tuberculosis Hospital Report (1910).

Chapter Seven: Pg. 101- Haines Photo Co. (1910); Pg. 107-Churchill Downs (1901) {{PD-old}}; Pg. 11o-Board of Tuberculosis Hospital Report (1908).

Chapter Eight: Pg. 115-Mark Ledford (markledford@gmail.com); Pg. 127-Mark Ledford (markledford@gmail.com); Pg. 128 CC Thomas (2007); Pg. 129-Mark Ledford (markledford@gmail.com); Pg. 130-Mark Ledford (markledford@gmail.com); Pg. 131-Bottom-Waverly Hope Foundation (1996); Page 132-CC Thomas (2007); Page 133-Sketch from Waverly Hope Foundation (1996).

Chapter Nine-Pg. 134-Board of Tuberculosis Hospital Report (1910); Pg. 135-Board of Tuberculosis Hospital Report (1910); Pg. 136-University of Louisville Archives; Pg. 139-Board of Tuberculosis Hospital Report (1910); Pg. 143-Board of Tuberculosis Hospital Report (1910).

Chapter Ten: Pg. 150-Board of Tuberculosis Hospital Report (1910); Pg. 153-Board of Tuberculosis Hospital Report (1910); Pg. 156-W. Marsh (2006).

Chapter Eleven: Pg. 157-CC Thomas (2007); Pg. 158-Mark Ledford (markledford@gmail.com); Pg. 159-Mark Ledford (markledford@gmail.com); Pg. 160-Mark Ledford (markledford@gmail.com); Pg. 161-Mark Ledford (markledford@gmail.com); Pg. 163-Mark Ledford (markledford@gmail.com); Pg. 165-Mark Ledford (markledford@gmail.com).

**The author is indebted to various individuals who shared stories and clippings, too numerous to mention. The author also has referenced these

Chapter Four: Pg. 49-Board of Tuberculosis Hospital Report (1910); Page 52-Board of Tuberculosis Hospital Report (1908); Page 53-Board of Tuberculosis Hospital Report (1910); Pg. 60-University of Louisville Archives (1926); Pg. 62-University of Louisville Archives.

Chapter Five: Pg. 65-University of Louisville Archives; Pg. 66 and 67-University of Louisville Archives; Pg. 79- Louisville Tuberculosis Association (1927); Pg. 80-American Lung Association Christmas Seal (1927).

Chapter Six: Pg. 84-University of Louisville Archives; Pg. 86-University of Louisville Archives; Pg. 88 -Board of Tuberculosis Hospital Report (1908); Pg. 89-Rene Laennec (1825) {{PD-old}}; Pg. 91-University of Louisville Archives; Pg. 93-Board of Tuberculosis Hospital Report (1910).

Chapter Seven: Pg. 101- Haines Photo Co. (1910); Pg. 107-Churchill Downs (1901) {{PD-old}}; Pg. 11o-Board of Tuberculosis Hospital Report (1908).

Chapter Eight: Pg. 115-Mark Ledford (markledford@gmail.com); Pg. 127-Mark Ledford (markledford@gmail.com); Pg. 128 CC Thomas (2007); Pg. 129-Mark Ledford (markledford@gmail.com); Pg. 130-Mark Ledford (markledford@gmail.com); Pg. 131-Bottom-Waverly Hope Foundation (1996); Page 132-CC Thomas (2007); Page 133-Sketch from Waverly Hope Foundation (1996).

Chapter Nine-Pg. 134-Board of Tuberculosis Hospital Report (1910); Pg. 135-Board of Tuberculosis Hospital Report (1910); Pg. 136-University of Louisville Archives; Pg. 139-Board of Tuberculosis Hospital Report (1910); Pg. 143-Board of Tuberculosis Hospital Report (1910).

Chapter Ten: Pg. 150-Board of Tuberculosis Hospital Report (1910); Pg. 153-Board of Tuberculosis Hospital Report (1910); Pg. 156-W. Marsh (2006).

Chapter Eleven: Pg. 157-CC Thomas (2007); Pg. 158-Mark Ledford (markledford@gmail.com); Pg. 159-Mark Ledford (markledford@gmail.com); Pg. 160-Mark Ledford (markledford@gmail.com); Pg. 161-Mark Ledford (markledford@gmail.com); Pg. 163-Mark Ledford (markledford@gmail.com); Pg. 165-Mark Ledford (markledford@gmail.com).

**The author is indebted to various individuals who shared stories and clippings, too numerous to mention. The author also has referenced these newspapers for some information and credit is hereby given due to *The Courier-Journal, The Louisville Herald, The Louisville Post, The Louisville Herald-Post* and *The Louisville Times*.

**Waverly Media Presentations**
*Tuberculosis in Retreat* (1938 Documentary)
*On the Firing Line* (Documentary)
ABC/Fox's Family Channel *Scariest Places on Earth* (2001 Documentary Episode)
VH1's *Celebrity Paranormal Project* (2006 Reality Show Episode)
SciFi Channel's *Ghost Hunters* (2006 Documentary Episode)
Terror Normal's *Episode 1: The Ghosts of Waverly Hills Sanatorium* (2007 Documentary)

**Waverly Print References (Fiction and Nonfiction)**
*The Encyclopedia of Louisville* by John Kleber
*Ghosthunting Kentucky: America's Haunted Roadtip* by Patti Starr and John Kachuba
*Pandemonium* by Christopher Bec
*The Requiem Rose: A Waverly Hills Story* by James Markert
*Sanitorium: Webster's Timeline History, 1801-2007* by Icon Group International
*Spookiest Stories Ever: Four Seasons of Kentucky's Ghosts* by Roberta Simpson Brown et. al.
*A Tuberculosis Directory Containing a List of Institutions, Associations and Other Agencies* by National Tuberculosis Association
*Weird Kentucky: Your Travel Guide to Kentucky's Local Legends and Best Kept Secrets* by Jeffrey Holland et.al.
*A White Wind Blew: A Novel of Waverly Hills* by James Markert

Made in the USA
Charleston, SC
02 May 2013